Contents

Introduction

Congratulations, Mama, you have taken the first step toward awareness, clarity, and acceptance by opening this book. Welcome. If you were sitting across the table from us, we would hand you a cup of coffee, look you in the eye, and share a hug, laughter, and tears. We are a part of a unique club, one that you possibly chose if you adopted or one that you didn't. You joined this club when you stepped into the world of special needs, additional needs, or different abilities (whatever the newest acceptable label is at the moment). The truth is we don't necessarily want to embrace the labels, and that's okay. Your identity shouldn't be based on your child's diagnoses or lack thereof, but we acknowledge how your situation has changed you and continually shapes you. (If you are not a special needs mom, keep reading; we have a message for you also.)

Mothers like us experience a complicated array of emotions such as fear, disappointment, guilt, anger, grief, and despair. We are burned out, exhausted, grieving the healthy child (either mentally or physically) we do not have, and yearning for relief. We feel isolated and experience jealousy and feelings of inadequacy when we look at others' situations. Wrestling in our relationship with God, we struggle with guilt over what we might have done to deserve this, anger for the seemingly endless trials, and despair over what the future will hold. You are not alone, and this book is for you.

This book shares the messy emotions that come with the journey of a special needs mom and how to navigate them. We agree that feelings are complicated. We aren't offering cliché solutions but rather ways to wrestle with and through them. Rarely is any challenging experience wrapped up like a beautiful Christmas package from a department store. Emotions are not an either/or situation but rather a both/and. You can be sorrowful yet know peace from God's presence. You can grieve and still be grateful.

We are three special needs moms with over thirty years of experience raising children with medical, mental, and special emotional needs. Amy began her journey through adoption, hidden disabilities, and mental health issues. Carrie's son was prenatally diagnosed with a permanently disabling condition and became medically fragile after birth, facing over sixty surgeries throughout his lifetime (so far). Sara's son received a terminal diagnosis at age nine, and she and her family members are determined not to let the diagnosis define the quality of their lives.

This book dives into the other side of special, the other side of parenting a special needs child that is difficult to talk about: the messy emotions that aren't ever fixed. They only lie dormant for a while like plants under winter snow blanketing the earth until spring's thaw comes and draws them to life. This book is a guide for you to navigate this messy, emotional, joy-filled life. It's intentionally crafted, so you don't need to read it cover to cover. You may, but we know your time and attention are limited. Pick up this book and start at chapter 9 if you wish. It's okay (especially if you're type A like us) to start where you need the most help. If you have a day when you're struggling with guilt, read that chapter. Each chapter introduces the difficult emotion and leads you through a series of three authors' thoughts, experiences, and perspectives. Then the chapter closes with a Bible verse of encouragement and reflective questions to ponder so you can take practical steps toward acceptance and clarity.

Rarely is any book written in a vacuum, and while we were writing this one, each of us dealt with various crises with our children. It made us realize that this is probably true of your life also, so we wrote a bonus chapter on navigating crises when they arise. We pray it blesses you. It's both practical and spiritual.

If you're reading this and you are a spouse, sibling, family member, friend, ministry leader, or you just know a mom with a special needs child, we welcome you. You will gain fantastic insight into what moms deal with, a small glimpse into their daily lives, and ideas on how you can support them. Clarity is kindness; the more you understand, the more empathy you can show. Thank you for taking the time to read this book.

When we (Amy, Carrie, and Sara) met through a writing group, we realized that even though our stories of parenting special needs children were vastly different, we could relate to one another's feelings of doubt, fear, guilt, and grief. So we started a podcast (*Take Heart Special Moms*) to connect with other moms in similar situations and to encourage them. For some reason, in the subculture of special needs parenting, there seems to be an unspoken competition of "my child is worse off than yours." While it is accurate that our traumatic experiences are our own and no one else's, it's time to reach out to one another and build on what we have in common. We share the loss of a dream of what we expected out of life. We are learning to deal with the roller-coaster ride of thoughts and emotions. We need connection with Jesus and with one another.

Our experiences might differ, but we can relate because of our common feelings. We pray that something from our stories will help you take just one step toward growing in faith, hope, joy, and connection.

We are honored that you have this book in your hands, and we pray it is a blessing. May reading it be like sitting together at a table sharing hearts so you are heard, understood, and encouraged. You are seen. You are known. You are loved.

1

Loneliness to Connection

Feeling lonely is a common and painfully familiar emotion for special needs moms. Leaving the home can often be exponentially more difficult simply because our child's needs are too difficult to manage in new places and the lack of accessibility seems insurmountable. Too often, though, our own belief that no one will understand (or care) about our situation keeps us home. There are also times when we feel judged or like we are being measured with some sort of special needs mom success stick, and we're coming up short. So we isolate ourselves. We don't know how to effectively cope with ongoing loneliness and isolation.

We know as Christians that God is always with us, yet that doesn't eliminate the need for human relationships. We want to move to a place of authentic connection, but when we are running low on time, energy, and ideas, how do we battle our negative thoughts and reach out to others?

When I (Amy) was pregnant with our first baby, my husband and I moved to Cleveland, Ohio. I didn't know one person and was very lonely. I decided to sign up for a prenatal exercise class. When I arrived, there was one other person there. Her name was Jen.

She had recently moved to the area and was also pregnant with her first baby. We started chatting. We have kept that conversation going for twenty-eight years, and she is one of my dearest friends. We have raised kids together, laughed until we cried, and vacationed together. She wiped tears off my face in a dirty gas station bathroom when I thought I was having a miscarriage. She drove from Ohio to Michigan to clean my house and cook for me when my dad died suddenly. I helped her get through her daughter's wedding. A year later, she helped me get through my son's wedding.

We have done life together. But there was a time in my life when I shut her out. I believed the lie that she would not understand my life. So many times in the past several years, I have felt judged, misunderstood, and helpless. Underlying all these feelings is the isolation and loneliness of being in a unique parenting situation.

Parenting a special needs child can be very isolating. I didn't know anyone who understood this unique road we were walking, so I didn't talk about it. Few people walk this same path, which makes it hard to share worries and feelings. We are afraid of being misunderstood, so we isolate ourselves.

As special needs moms the demands of our lives make it difficult to connect. We may also feel lonely because we are constantly feeling misunderstood. We may find the courage to open up to someone, but they just don't get it. Our friends try to offer helpful advice, but sometimes those comments hurt and leave us feeling lonelier.

After countless situations of feeling unheard and misunderstood, our loneliness can become a shield. We don't want to trust others or let them in. Feeling lonely and isolated can make us feel like we are standing out in the cold and away from all that is warm and nourishing.

As a mom, I was overwhelmed with the needs of our family. I was trying to help our daughter, keep the rest of the family afloat, and just survive. The story I was telling myself was I was failing as a mom and no one could possibly understand my life. I assumed everyone was judging me.

The loop of lies running in my head caused me to isolate myself from someone who loves me. I had shared our struggles with Jen, but she was always quick to give me solutions. Instead of being clear and telling her I did not want solutions, I assumed she did not understand and decided to tell her less.

My husband and I were struggling to parent a child with reactive attachment disorder (RAD) and fetal alcohol spectrum disorder (FASD). As her behaviors continued to escalate, we made the difficult and heartbreaking decision to place her in a therapeutic boarding school. We realized we could not help her and that she needed a different environment.

We knew this was best for our family, even though I felt like I was failing our child. I dreaded telling others. Soon after that, Jen and her family came for a visit. I needed to tell her of our decision, and I remember that day very clearly. We were sitting on a park bench on a beautiful Michigan summer day. I started to open up to her about what was happening in our home and explained why we were making the painful decision to send our child to a treatment facility. Instead of the judgment I was expecting, my dear friend spoke life-giving words of grace, love, and compassion. She told me how much she wanted to support me. She expressed her deep sadness for me. Jen had never shown me anything but love and kindness. But the lies that kept running in my head and my mom-guilt made me assume she would judge me.

The lies we believe about ourselves cause us to forget what we know to be true. They skew our perspective. Loneliness and isolation cause us to forget that we are made for connection and can hurt the relationships we hold most dear.

I was trying so hard to fix a situation I could not fix. I had fallen deep into a pit of mom-guilt. I allowed my negative thoughts to isolate me. I forgot this truth: Jen was for the well-being of my entire family. But most of all, she was in my corner. After that day, I started to breathe. I allowed myself to open up to those in my life.

The lies we believe about ourselves cause us to forget what we know to be true.

Maybe you are feeling isolated and overwhelmed by your life. Maybe you think no one will understand. Here is what I want you to know: you are not alone. What can you do to move from loneliness to connection?

First of all, take your loneliness to God. He cares so much for you, and he made you for connection and fellowship. You are never abandoned or unseen by God. He sees you and knows you in every moment. Ask him to give you the courage to reach out to and connect with others. Pray for people to come into your life who can walk this road with you.

16

Next, find one person you can talk to, and tell them what you need. Do not let limiting beliefs stop you from connection with a friend. You may need to wipe the slate clean of all your preconceived ideas of friendship. You may need to ask God to help you heal from past hurts. Be brave, reach out, be persistent, and look for invitations and opportunities to connect.

The loved ones in your life will never know you're lonely or what you need if you do not tell them. Reaching out will help you breathe and give you the strength to go on. We are not meant to walk this road alone; we need each other. We are made to connect.

Moms who struggle with loneliness may assume they can't make friends due to the all-consuming needs at home. As they prepare for another surgery or load the car to head out for their child's therapy, they give up on forming relationships outside the family because their role consumes too much energy, time, and freedom. There's little mental energy left to figure out how to connect with others. Besides, it's easy to imagine other women aren't interested in spending time with an overwhelmed special needs mom. What if the problem isn't our circumstances? What if it's our limiting belief that no one will understand or care about our situation? How do we battle that mindset and open up to a life of fulfilling connection?

My (Carrie's) son has a condition that is one of the most common permanently disabling congenital conditions in the United States. Thousands of parents are in the same situation, yet I have felt alone. After he was born, he went into respiratory failure and needed a trach, ventilator, and feeding tube. We found ourselves dealing with medical experiences that were rare for his condition. I felt alone because his diagnosis wasn't just like that of others, but we didn't fit elsewhere either.

I am a self-proclaimed connector who needs validation from others to feel accepted and wanted. If and when that doesn't happen, I switch to comparison mode, examining how my child's diagnosis is more complex than that of others and how I perform as his mother. My son has played Miracle League Baseball and sled hockey and has participated in Special Olympics. I have found in these circles that special needs parents are reticent to reach out to one another and connect. But we should be one another's best cheerleaders, encouragers, and confidants. How do we get there? If you find yourself in this same situation, how do you overcome the loneliness that is so often a part of our world?

First, choose connection over competition. Instead of sitting in a doctor's office mentally comparing your situation to someone else's to determine whether you're better or worse off than the family next to you, ask yourself, How can we connect? What do we have in common?

I often think of the story of Mary and Elizabeth in Scripture. Both of them were pregnant, expecting unique babies. Elizabeth, further along, could have been jealous over the fact that Mary was chosen to carry the Messiah. After all, what did Mary know about being the mother to the Savior at such a young age? Why wasn't she (Elizabeth) chosen? In turn, Mary could have chosen not to visit this much older cousin, who was carrying only the forerunner of the Messiah. Instead, they chose connection over competition. After the angel left Mary, Luke tells us that she "hurried to a town in the hill country" to be with her cousin (Luke 1:39). Can you imagine the stories and experiences they shared?

Children with the same diagnosis are like snowflakes. No two special needs children are exactly the same. A saying in the autism community is "If you've met one person with autism, then you've met one person with autism." This is true about all diagnoses and situations. Instead of competing with other moms over who has the worst-case scenario, search for what you have in common. Our emotions and needs are similar. We have similar desires and dreams for our children as well as similar fears.

A few years after our son was born, I decided to start my own in-person support group with a friend who was in a similar situation when we couldn't find a place to fit in and be understood. We built on our common ground, and those years were filled with connection instead of loneliness. The one thing we had in common was that our children were medically fragile. Once we started, others were drawn to us, and we realized we could help one another. Sometimes the best resources mothers have are other parents! As our children have become teenagers, it's been more challenging to keep up with monthly meetings, but recently one of the moms reached out to let me know how much our group helped her during those early years.

Choose connection over competition.

You never know the impact you can have when you choose connection over competition. So reach out to others. Ask the Lord to give you the support and connection you need. When the angel revealed to Mary that she was expecting, he gave her the precious gift of connection by sharing the news that Elizabeth was also pregnant. In both situations (old age and virginity), they shared the truth that nothing is impossible with God. God created you for connection.

Second, extend your hand. Friendships begin when we look for ways to bless others. There are times when we need to be on the receiving end—of meals, help, and support. However, there may be other moments when we can extend our hand to help others through prayer, a shoulder to cry on, or a listening ear.

When Mary arrived at Elizabeth's house, Elizabeth was filled with the Holy Spirit and spoke a blessing over Mary. She spoke the truth into her life that she was blessed among women. Afterward, Mary prayed a prayer of worship. When we encourage one another, that is worship to God. When we comfort others with the comfort God has comforted us with, that is connection. Never think that extending your hand has to be something significant like starting a nonprofit or raising money for a cause. Simple acts can make a big difference and create lifelong connections.

Finally, connect with God. Only God can truly fulfill every longing of our hearts. Often in our pain, we tend to push him away. Instead of retreating, lean into the One who desires a relationship with you. How do you connect with your Creator daily when you're overwhelmed and exhausted? Choose one thing to do today and do it. Write out a verse of encouragement and put it on your mirror. Pray over your child while caring for them. You don't have to do something that takes an hour or even fifteen minutes. Start with just a few minutes, communicate with the One who understands your deepest longings and needs, and build a relationship with him. He is the One who will never fail you. He will always be with you and so strongly desired to have a relationship (connection) with you that he left heaven and came to earth as a helpless infant to be your Immanuel, "God with us."

An unrelenting, never-ending to-do list often surrounds us as special needs moms. Some of us are literally never physically alone because we are our child's hands, feet, and even voice. Some of us are rarely physically alone because we can't take the chance of our child being alone. Whatever the reason, whatever the diagnosis, we rarely get a moment just to be who we are or do what we desire. When we do, we have those moments when it hits us that we don't have the same concerns as those around us, whether they are friends, family, or strangers. We feel out of place. We feel alone. We feel isolated.

Perhaps we take our child to an activity only to find out it is not accessible. My (Sara's) church is lovingly referred to in our community as the city set on a hill. This is taken from Scripture, and we are literally set on a large hill. Attending church functions isn't always simple. Our church has been around for years and has expanded to multiple levels, but it isn't always the easiest to maneuver for those with physical limitations or disabilities.

Once we attended an outdoor church function, but both of the accessible entrances were closed off for safety reasons. They didn't want people driving through and endangering others. But the staff and volunteers ended up blocking what were the only accessible entrances to this activity for those with disabilities. My husband and I eventually moved all the cones and barriers, drove through, and then put them back. When we kindly mentioned what happened to those in charge, they were extremely apologetic and said they had made sure the building door was accessible. They didn't think of how those with physical disabilities would get into the building.

Another time we decided to attend a function at the last minute. When we arrived, we found that our son couldn't physically do the planned activities. The response was innocent enough. We were told they were glad our son was there, but since they thought he wasn't going to come, they didn't plan activities for him. Those experiences left us feeling like an imposition. We felt alone and isolated.

You may not struggle with accessibility. Your child may struggle with sensory overload or behavioral issues. You see the discomfort or even the pity in others. To avoid a repeat, you aren't invited back, or you avoid new things altogether. Even though you don't necessarily blame others for their reactions, you feel disconnected and lack vital human relationships.

Sometimes we turn to other moms with children with special needs only to realize we rarely have moments when we can sit down together and chat. When we do chat, we discuss insurance appeals, education issues, bullies at school, or any of the many obstacles we deal with on a daily basis. Before we know it, we have no substantial connections.

Maybe we turn to online support groups. It is the digital era, we have the world at our fingertips, and anyone can find a group, right? But then we struggle to find a group that fits our needs. That's when we begin to give up. That's when the loneliness stops shadowing us and begins to shroud us in darkness. The lonelier we are, the more we are convinced our situation won't ever change.

But things can change. Authentic connection can be found. It may not look like we had hoped. It may not be like other moms' connections. And that's okay. To battle loneliness at its core, first look to God. Work at having a meaningful connection with him.

I grew up a Christian, but after my son's diagnosis, I realized that I didn't really know God. I knew the God who was to be feared, and I knew the God who was all-knowing, but I didn't know the God who was a friend and confidant. I decided I needed to make an effort to carve out time to consistently be in the Word. One morning I decided God and I were going to spend some quality time together. I have to say that it ended up being the equivalent of an awkward first date. There I sat in my quiet nook with my Bible and a cup of coffee. I had even brushed my teeth and had on my best pajamas. I spent the first few minutes staring at the Bible and sipping my coffee. I realized that I should have prepared more and brought a devotional or reading plan. I was already there, so I decided to make the most of our time together.

Since it was just God, me, my Bible, and a cup of coffee, I decided to start a conversation, but I had no idea what to say or where to begin. I was petrified that he would realize I was unfiltered and awkward. He was going to realize I had no idea what I was doing. I had been going through the church motions for years, but for all intents and purposes, I was new to this relationship. And I was lost. However, the more I stuck with this new relationship, the more I realized he wasn't going anywhere (despite my awkwardness).

I now find comfort in knowing just how accepting, faithful, and present God always is. He loves me, which makes it easier to love myself. He appreciates my desire to learn more about him. James 4:8 says, "Draw near to God, and he will draw near to you" (ESV). You are never truly alone, and the more you learn about God, the more you'll begin to see and feel him in your life.

Second, just like working at getting to know God, work at getting to know others. We need to stop assuming that no one "gets us." They'll never understand us if we don't share anything with them. Likewise, we'll never understand them if we don't listen. It is vital not only to notice our differences but also to highlight them. Our child with special needs has shown us beauty and unity in diversity, right? Let's start practicing that in each of our relationships.

Third, to battle loneliness, help others. The lonelier we become, the easier it is for us to believe that no one understands hardship as we do. This is the perfect recipe to begin wallowing in a victim's mentality. But as we serve others, we begin to see that we haven't cornered the market on despair, hardship, and loneliness. As corny and cliché as it sounds, it's true that when we help others, we help ourselves. But how do we serve others when we are running low on money and time ourselves? We send a note or email to a friend or someone we just met (maybe a friend yet to be). We volunteer for something we can do with our child. We pick up a few extra school supplies and take them to a local public school. We keep it simple. Remember, generosity is generosity to God.

Remember the church function that had the accessible entrances blocked for safety? I'm not going to lie. I was upset and frustrated in that moment. After thinking about it, I knew our church had our best interest at heart. Our church leaders and volunteers simply didn't realize the problem. They had many moving parts to think of, and they didn't know what they didn't know. It was in that moment I realized that they were never going to understand until we shared our needs with them. There is a reason why it takes a multitude of volunteers to plan for events. One or two staff members or volunteers can't think of everything.

Along with another couple, my husband and I started a special needs ministry at our church. Several years later, staff, leaders, and volunteers seek our input when planning events. Serving others has brought us connection while ensuring our needs are being met. We are also advocating for our children while educating others. The more we share our needs, show our vulnerability, and strive to help others, the more we can make and grow authentic connections.

You are worth getting to know. Never forget that.

Reflections

When you pass through the waters,
   I will be with you;
and when you pass through the rivers,
   they will not sweep over you.
When you walk through the fire,
   you will not be burned;
   the flames will not set you ablaze. (Isa. 43:2)

1. What is one thing you can do today to remind yourself that you are worth knowing?
2. In what way can you let someone clearly know what you need? How can you more clearly communicate how someone can serve you well?
3. Reflect on Isaiah 43:2 and list the waters you are passing through. Ask God to help you so they don't sweep

over you. List the fires of your life and ask God to protect you from the flames. God is already right there with you waiting to shoulder it all. Turn to him. Connect with him.

4. What situations make you feel lonely? What is one thing you can do today to choose connection with another mom in a situation similar to yours?

2

Grief to Hope

Grief or the grieving cycle is most often associated with losing a loved one, not with being a special needs mom. However, grief is an often overlooked but essential part of the special needs journey. It's grief not over the loss of a person but rather over the loss of the dream of having a healthy, able-bodied child, either mentally or physically. It's the sorrow over life not turning out as you expected. The first time we came across this concept was in a book titled *Extraordinary Kids: Nurturing and Championing Your Child with Special Needs*. The authors relate what nurse Joanne Woosley says to parents whose newborn babies are born with Down syndrome: "You have to grieve for the child you were expecting before you can accept the child you have."[1]

Some stages of grief you might experience are:

- **Denial:** I can't believe this is happening to me.
- **Anxiety:** How can I possibly handle this?

- **Fear:** What will happen to my child and my family?
- **Guilt:** What did I do to cause this?
- **Depression:** My hopes and dreams seem to be lost forever.
- **Anger:** This isn't fair!
- **Acceptance:** I don't like what has happened. I don't understand why it happened. I don't know how I'm going to handle this. But God knows, and I can trust him.[2]

As our journeys have continued, one vital lesson we've learned is that the grieving cycle is something we experience not once but repeatedly. The cycle isn't linear either; just because you have feelings of denial doesn't mean anxiety automatically follows. We often bounce around among these emotions.

Grief happens the day you send your child to preschool and realize they lag behind their peers. It hits you again after a significant medical event or when you have to make tough decisions about your child. The moments we acknowledged and accepted that grief was a continual part of parenting were freeing.

In life, it's nice to know what to expect. Understanding that the reason you went off on the barista at Starbucks was not necessarily because your order was incorrect but rather because of the chaotic events of the past week is essential. As we process grief, we can spot it spilling into other parts of life; even if we can't stop the outburst, we can trace it back to the cause.

Feelings of sadness and grief are sneaky, but healing begins when you understand the need to grieve the unexpected, the "not measuring up" moments of this journey as a special needs mom.

A few years ago, we moved into a new house. After we settled in, I (Amy) started exploring the yard. I was excited to see three mature lilac bushes already planted and blooming. Lilacs are my favorite flower.

I was delighted with those bushes. I was not the one who planted and watered them, hoping they would grow. I showed up at this new house and enjoyed them. The following spring I was anticipating the lilacs to bloom. I kept checking them, but the branches were bare. Nothing. Not even a little green shoot. I was hoping they were late bloomers.

I started getting a tad bit obsessed. I started checking the progress of not just my own bushes but every lilac bush I saw in my neighborhood. It seemed that all three of mine were dead. I wanted them dug up immediately. I didn't want to look at dead bushes all summer. I thought about calling the nursery to buy the biggest bushes. I wanted the space filled and everything back to normal. I didn't want to wait for the new life to grow. All I could see was what was not there.

Life can be like this, especially when you've been handed a situation or diagnosis you were not expecting. Most of us did not anticipate being special needs moms. We resist looking at the elements of our lives that seem dead or different than we expected. When we finally open our eyes to reality, we want to rush in and fill the void with what we had hoped would grow there. We conclude new growth is going much slower than expected and struggle to find patience to watch a small thing grow, especially when it is not developing at the rate we had hoped for.

Parenting a child with mental health issues and reactive attachment disorder (RAD) has been like studying, even obsessing over, those lilac bushes. I had to learn to let my expectations die. I had dreams of what I thought our family would be like when we adopted our child. I dreamed of a relationship with her. I held on to that dead tree of my hopes and expectations for far too long. I tried to force growth, fix the relationship, and make it look like what I had anticipated it would be. I did not like looking at the empty space where a mother-child relationship should be.

We have to allow ourselves to grieve. Part of allowing ourselves to grieve is naming what we are grieving. We have a tendency to avoid grief by pushing it away and looking for solutions to fix what is wrong. We do this because grief is difficult; no one wants to grieve. As a special needs mom, you may feel too overwhelmed even to give space to what you need to grieve. We often are too busy even to recognize what we need. But grief is essential. Please allow yourself to grieve the way you need to.

We also have expectations put on us to look on the bright side and to count our blessings, especially in the world of Christian faith. We believe in hope and resurrection. Those are the tenets of our faith, so it is easy to be uncomfortable when life is challenging.

We should count our blessings, of course. But we also have to allow ourselves to grieve and know that grief is good as well. God can handle where you are right now. You can tell him what grieves your heart, your disappointments and hurts, and he will be there with you. You can take it all to God. He is the God of comfort (2 Cor. 1:3–5). God can handle whatever you say to him, and he does not leave you.

So give yourself permission to grieve. Try not to hustle it away with happy thoughts, plans for how to fix things, or general busyness and distractions. Once you give yourself permission to name what you're grieving, you can start the slow process of embracing the reality of what is.

Once I learned to accept what it looks like to parent a child with trauma and attachment issues, I realized I needed to step back and watch the growth. Some spots are green and blooming; other spots are empty. None of it looks like I thought it would. I cannot force growth or change what is growing. What I can do is welcome what is and appreciate the beauty. This process is not easy, and I am still in the midst of it, but it is necessary.

Naming what you're grieving doesn't mean you're a bad mom or that you love your child any less. It makes you a brave mom and allows you to move forward and accept what is. Without honest grief, there's no way to move forward toward hope.

True hope ties us to God.

Grief will always be a part of our lives as special needs moms, but we cannot forget to hope. Sometimes we abound in hope, and sometimes hope ties us to an outcome, like hoping test results come back negative. But true hope ties us to God; true hope allows us to feel seen, held, and loved. Hope is what anchors us to God.

This is not the kind of hope we can make up or conjure up by willpower. This hope rests in the person of Jesus, and we get to open our hearts and receive it. This hope does not depend on a particular outcome or external circumstances. This hope is rooted in the truest of all truth: Christ loves us.

We can bring our sorrows to God and ask for eyes to see his goodness in the midst of what is breaking our hearts. This is when we start to notice his love, his grace, and the signs of hope around us.

We can look for the invitation to hope in things outside our special needs child. We can find hope in the friends who are there for us, the meals left on our doorstep, the sun on our faces, the first signs of spring, and the prayers whispered in the dark for us.

These little sips of grace and hope on your parched throat will give you the strength to walk this journey.

⁓

The day my (Carrie's) grieving cycle began was when my unborn baby received his diagnosis. It was the day I became a "special needs mom." I remember not wanting that label. Well-meaning friends tried to connect me with other parents who had children with the same diagnosis, but I didn't want any part of it. "Special needs" was a club I wasn't ready to join.

Denial, anger, frustration, fear, sadness, and grief are common emotions we experience when life doesn't turn out the way we expect. Moving from grief to hope doesn't mean we've left sorrow far behind or that we'll never experience it again. It means holding the complex emotions together, acknowledging that life is hard, yet drawing near to God, believing he is near to us.

Hope can be difficult to define. In his podcast, *The Place We Find Ourselves*, Adam Young defines hope as groaning inwardly while waiting expectantly. Hope holds two things together—the hope that God will satisfy our longings and the groaning when they go unfulfilled.[3] The weight of unfulfilled longings can weigh us down. So what do we do with those unmet expectations? We lament and we expect grief through-out our journey.

Several years into our special needs journey, God graciously revealed to me that grief would be an ongoing part of it. When we faced each medical event, I would buck up and put on my game face so I could advocate for what my son needed and make life-saving medical decisions. I portrayed a facade of strength so he wouldn't have to handle my grief. I shut off my emotions entirely because I thought it was up to me to bring him home whole and safe (which is completely false). I didn't realize that grief would come bubbling up to the surface days, weeks, and months later. A seemingly insignificant event like Chick-fil-A incorrectly filling my order brought a torrent of tears. That was grief. I had not allowed the time or space to lament previous events, emotions, and challenging situations.

When emotions come, stop and think about what is trigger-ing them. Ask yourself some questions. Has your child had a recent hospital stay? Has your child missed a milestone that your friend's child is achieving right now? Have you missed some much-needed alone time? What is today's date? Is it an anniversary of a prior time of trauma? Our brains may not remember, but our bodies do. It's called implicit memory. So name the emotion, and then think about the source. There is kindness in clearly defining our emotions and the reasons behind them.

After you've identified the source of your emotions (this first step does require some practice and awareness), you need to allow time and space to lament. Do not feel guilty for griev-ing for a child who is still living. Do not allow people who have lost children to dismiss your feelings. Our feelings are valid and a natural part of this journey, and lament brings us closer to the heart of God. It's okay to be sad and even angry that we live in a world that groans under the effects of sin.

In Scripture, Job is someone we often recognize as one who experienced significant loss. When I read his conversations with God about his agony and pain, I often wonder how he was able to talk to God like that. He raged against God. He cursed the day of his birth. He lamented his situation. At the end of the book, we are surprised to find that God tells Job's friend Eliphaz that only Job had spoken rightly about God (Job 42:7). How is that possible? Perhaps because Job dared to lament and be honest with God about his feelings. He expressed his sorrow and mourned deeply. Authentic relationships require honesty and transparency. A relationship with God isn't any different. He wants us to have the courage to tell him what we feel.

What are some ways to lament? First of all, there's no script for lament. I mourn difficulties through listening to music. I experience a cathartic release when I cry out to God in song. Another way to lament is through journaling. It's challenging to describe (in writing) what we are thinking and feeling—to see it in black ink on white paper, so bold and clear—but the written word can clarify thoughts and emotions.

Reading the Psalms and praying them to God is another way to lament. When we read the psalms of David, we find the raw emotions of grief, sadness, and anger. David cried out repeatedly that he felt God wasn't listening to him, that he had turned his back on him. David was honest about his pain. At the end of many chapters, we might notice that some of his rantings turn to praise and thankfulness. This might seem like a contradiction, but David was a poet and a songwriter. Those psalms were probably not written in an hour or a day. They were most likely written over an extended period of processing, grieving, wrestling with the difficulties of his situation, crying out in his grief, and then remembering who God is. As we mourn, we can choose to lean into God's comfort and love instead of running away.

In the sorrow of a challenging situation, take time to remember the character of God and reflect on his promises. "The LORD is close to the brokenhearted and saves those who are crushed in spirit" (Ps. 34:18). Look back at your life and list all the times God has been faithful, what he's revealed about his character, and how he has provided. Such things can remind you that he loves you and is near. He hasn't ever left. He will never leave you nor forsake you.

As you attempt to move toward hope in your grief, imagine this. Close your eyes and imagine a sepia-colored landscape of trees, grass, flowers, the sun, and a cloudless sky. In our grief, we know the true colors of the world (the sun shines against a blue sky, the trees and grass are bright green, and the flowers are arrayed in bright pink, purple, red, and yellow), but they are hard to see. Like with the original televisions, all we can see are shades of black, white, and gray. But as we lament and turn our sorrows over to our Savior, the colors appear. They begin in the far-left corner of our lives and spread from one side to the other, transforming the dull monotone into beautiful, vibrant color. When we grieve with hope, God is faithful to renew the vision we had about our lives, painting with his brush a wide array of colors we didn't imagine. Our lives might not be as we pictured, but they can be enriching and fulfilling.

Before my (Sara's) son's diagnosis, I had always associated grief with death. My son has complex medical issues, and his diagnosis is degenerative and terminal. But since he was alive when others had already succumbed to the disease, I didn't feel like I had the right to grieve.

But death doesn't have sole rights over grief. More times than not, grief is about the end of or the change in something familiar, desired, or even expected. So when we realized our little family's dream had abruptly changed, we experienced a range of emotions—most of which we didn't know how to name. I had no idea at the time, but the primary emotion I was feeling was grief.

The experts say grief has stages: denial, anger, bargaining, depression, and ultimately acceptance. I don't disagree. Perhaps for some people or situations, that is how grief works. I just feel that grief—ongoing and raw—can be more like an emotional funnel than an organized chart of stages. As moms to those with disabilities or special needs, we are faced with a diagnosis (or several) so unfamiliar and even unwanted that we are caught off guard. We are left with feelings we don't know how to name, let alone process. Being caught off guard never really stops, does it? There are surprises and obstacles around every corner, whether educational challenges, medical issues, or complications navigating daily life. It causes a heap of emotions.

All the feelings flood the emotional funnel at once with no rhyme or reason. Emotions we didn't realize we had pour out of our hearts. Denial drops in, followed closely by shock. Anger sloshes in and even splashes out and stains those standing too close. Depression drips in slowly, but there's a lot of it, so we carry it alone until it's too much to shoulder.

Pouring into the funnel never stops. Too many emotions are associated with the daily activities of being a caregiver for this process ever to stop. It's not like we reach a quota of hardship and heartache, and then we're finished. As parents or caregivers of someone with disabilities or special needs, we aren't exempt from "typical" difficulties such as financial issues, marital strains, job woes, or busy schedules. However, once we recognize the funnel is there, we can learn to use it to channel our emotions and process them.

Along with the anger, denial, shock, and depression, we realize we have a lot of determination, strength, resolve, and fortitude. As "good moms," we learn to hold on to those positive, strong feelings and keep them front and center. Those feelings are what we desire. Those feelings help us feel that we can actually survive this crazy life. Sure, the grief is still there; we just refuse to pour it into the emotional funnel anymore. And that works for a while. Eventually, though, the grief starts to overwhelm us and it has to go somewhere.

What if we poured everything we have into that emotional funnel? In goes the negative and the painful, along with the good and the positive. In goes the anger, but so does the determination. In goes the depression, but so does the fortitude to get out of bed and do it all over again. In go the questions we have for God, but so do our faith and trust in his promises. What begins to pour out of our hearts, and what does the funnel filter?

Amazingly enough, as we pour everything we have into that funnel (all the messy emotions), we realize that the negative feelings don't completely taint the positive ones. Sure, some of the bad leaks through and can have a negative effect on our overall emotional state, but ultimately what comes out of the filter at the bottom is genuinely beautiful—a blend of emotions that together are an accurate picture of our reality, our hearts, our spirits. It's real and it's powerful. What is poured out is hope.

At times, hope is a steady stream, and sometimes it's a trickle. Sometimes I even need to give the funnel a good shake or a solid whack to get the hope to start moving again.

At times, hope is a steady stream, and sometimes it's a trickle. Sometimes I even need to give the funnel a good shake or a solid whack to get the hope to start moving again.

At times, I honestly fear that my hope will run out. What happens if we run out of treatments? What happens if the constant fight for what our son needs doesn't ease up? What happens when I lose my child? What then? Will hope stop flowing? When I begin to anticipate grief yet to come, I remember Proverbs 23:18, which says: "For surely there is a hereafter, and your hope will not be cut off" (NKJV). I can take comfort knowing that my hope is not earthly driven but eternally granted. Hope is an unlimited resource given to us by our heavenly Father. We have the power to filter out the mess so the reward will freely flow.

If my earthly hope runs out, the source of hope does not. Jesus is hope. He is hope itself, and therefore our supply of hope never ends. Through Christ, hope is limitless and it is ours.

Reflections

So also you have sorrow now, but I will see you again, and your hearts will rejoice, and no one will take your joy from you. (John 16:22 ESV)

1. What would you want to tell Jesus if you could visibly see him next to you?
2. Think of a time when you recently felt disappointed. Name the grief that came along with that disappointment.
3. What events, places, or anniversary dates bring up feelings of grief? Write out a step-by-step plan right now for taking care of your body in those moments (steps of self-care) and resolve not to overschedule during those times.
4. What are some of God's comforting promises you can cling to while you're grieving? Write them on a note card and put them where they are visible. Check out these to get you started:
   - Your cries are heard: Psalm 40:1–3
   - You are not alone: Joshua 1:9
   - You have access to God's divine power: 2 Peter 1:3
   - God is near to you when your spirit is crushed: Psalm 34:18
   - God's mercies never end: Lamentations 3:22–24

3

Doubt to Faith

Most of us didn't anticipate being a special needs mom or all the challenges and unknowns that come with it. We have many questions along the way as we care for our child. For the most part, we can find answers to these daily questions as we search for the right doctor, treatment, or therapy. But what happens when those questions are about our faith and God?

How could he let our child go through this?

How could he let us go through this?

These questions stir up fear, uncertainty, and confusion. They also tempt us to isolate ourselves as we grapple with our doubts.

As Christians, we know that God is good, but moms often struggle to understand this in the midst of having a child with special needs. The pain and issues that come with our child can overwhelm us. How are we supposed to reconcile God's goodness with the difficulties?

We can find peace in the midst of our wavering faith.

We can realize God is with us and sees us as we face challenges.

We can trust God even in the midst of our doubts.

I (Amy) remember attending a Bible study years ago and hearing a teaching on Jeremiah 29:11: "'For I know the plans I have for you,' declares the LORD, 'plans to prosper you and not to harm you, plans to give you hope and a future.'" This verse is true. God does know our hearts and does have a plan for us. However, I remember sitting there and thinking that this meant nothing bad would happen to me. It says it right there in the Bible that I will prosper and not be harmed, and all I have to do is follow God by checking all the boxes. When life didn't turn out the way I thought it should, I tried harder, ran faster. I had moments when I was mad at God, but mostly I was mad at myself. I kept assuming that I just needed to do the right things and life would get better. I spent so much of my life being the "good girl," hoping that if I followed the rules, I would have an easier life. I tried to make my own way, doing the right things without true trust.

It's discouraging when life hands you something difficult and you feel like God has forgotten you. I struggled with this for years—this false idea that the promised blessing meant only nice things, problems solved, and issues disappearing. I later realized (and am still realizing) that I had missed the point. My walk with Christ had been focused on the scenery and the destination. If I did all the right things, life would be a pleasant ride and I would get to where I was supposed to be. I forgot over and over again that the journey is actually about my companion, Christ. He walks with me and loves me, and I am to follow him. I am always in his hands.

At times, I have allowed myself to be bitter about the difficult moments in my life. I have tried to figure out why God has allowed these things in my life. I want to know the purpose. But when I complain, obsess over my problems, and try to figure God out, I am not trusting God. Once again, I have missed the point. When I focus on the scenery and not my companion, all I can see are the valleys and the steep hills I have been asked to climb. When I stop and look at my companion, my perspective changes. God knows the plans he has for me; I am simply to follow.

I carried the burden of being a good girl, a good Christian, and a good special needs mom. In reality, following Christ means trusting him with my life, my plans, and my rules. I need to remember that I don't have to live life alone—he is with me every step of the way. I have not mastered this at all and still work on it every day. But following God's plans instead of my own is a much more peaceful way of walking through life.

Recently, someone asked me how God was working in the life of my daughter with special needs. After smiling politely and trying to come up with a good Christian answer, I went home and cried. I thought, *How is he working?*

Sometimes in our search for God, what we really want is not his will but our own. We have this idea that God showing up means healing and good results, all our worries and cares smoothed over and ready to be shared with the world in a rosy Instagram post. But guess what? God doesn't have to show up; he is already here. He's here in the mess and the stress, not just the posts we put on social media.

Our faith in God is about redemption, and redemption is continually present in our lives. We just have to look. We have to learn to accept that even in the midst of what doesn't make sense, God is good and provides what we need.

I know God has done many things in my life as a special needs mom. I may never know the true depth of his provision and grace. But I see glimpses of them every day. They rejuvenate me and help me to remember that he is always at my side, whether I am being the "good girl" or not.

The Bible tells the story of Hagar, the maidservant of Sarai and the mother to Abram's son Ishmael (you can read the story in Gen. 16). Hagar is being mistreated by Sarai, and she flees to the desert with her son. God comes to her and tells her to go back to Sarai, to go back to the difficult situation. He could have changed the situation, but instead he tells her to return to it.

What I love about this story is that Hagar says, "You are the God who sees me" (Gen. 16:13). God saw her. He did not change her situation, but she felt seen, and being seen gave her the strength to go back into the hard circumstances. This is what we need to remember. We are seen by God. He sits with us in our pain and doubt. Remember, too, that it is okay to doubt, to be mad, to cry on your bed, and to wonder what God is doing. He is still there and still sees you. He is continually working for your good, often in ways you will never know or see.

My hope for you today is that you will be able to find peace in your difficulties, that you will not feel guilty for struggling with faith, and that you will always remember that God sees you. I pray that you will know that you are God's beloved and that he is with you always.

By the time my (Carrie's) son Toby was five years old, he had had over ten surgeries and had been through almost six hundred hours of physical, occupational, and speech therapy. He had a feeding tube, a trach for breathing, and a ventilator at night for central sleep apnea. He was still trying to learn the skills of eating by mouth and speaking verbally.

That spring, life threw us another curveball. His shunt stopped working, which meant swelling in his brain that required surgery. The symptoms were subtle, and I almost missed them. One week later, in the early morning hours, he experienced his first seizure. We immediately jumped into action, called 911, and rushed him to the hospital. The seizure seemed to stop on the way, but once we arrived, it began again. This time he convulsively seized for so long that the doctors considered putting him under anesthesia. The multiple medications he was given didn't stop it. His body was so tired that we saw him only tremble, even though he was still convulsively seizing. Years before, I had placed seizures on the imaginary list of possible occurrences I never wanted to experience. I called it my "unbucket list." Now, I felt lost, alone, and overwhelmed. I doubted that God was near or knew what was happening to our son. After all, if he did, why would he allow such a thing to occur? Doubts about God's love, faithfulness, and nearness crept in.

Having been a Christ follower for some time, I had accepted long ago that trials were a part of life. I didn't doubt that God would do what was best for me, but the special needs journey is painful. At times, it feels too painful to bear. C. S. Lewis once said, "We are not necessarily doubting that God will do the best for us; we are wondering how painful the best will turn out to be."[1] This unexpected trial caused me to doubt that God was paying attention to our situation. It felt as if he was looking the other way. We were in an unexpected and terrifying medical crisis, unsure our son would wake again. I mistakenly believed that my faithfulness in the past negated future sorrow.

I mistakenly believed that my faithfulness in the past negated future sorrow.

Father Tim, in the novel *In This Mountain*, declares, "I'm ashamed to confess it, but I thought I knew my true worth to God, I thought my faithfulness had long ago been revealed to him. I didn't think he'd require anything more."[2] We had already been through five years of trials. I felt that I had already proven I could praise God in a storm, which meant we wouldn't have more trials. I didn't think he would expect any more from me. As I cried and prayed for God to answer me, a friend gently reminded me that God knew in advance this would happen. He had lovingly sifted it through his hands, and even though it was devastating, he was near. He was present. He hadn't looked the other way.

In seasons of doubt, we need to remember that God's faithfulness doesn't depend on our feelings about him or our situation. Doubting God's goodness is part of being human, especially when facing trauma. God does not turn away from us but invites us to let him in. One of my favorite quotes comes from the late husband of a fellow podcast host: "When you feel you cannot trust God's actions in your life, you must trust his heart."[3] Even if we can't understand God's purposes in our trials, we must trust his character. He cannot be anything but loving, trustworthy, kind, comforting, gracious, and merciful.

God cannot be separated from who he is. The truth is that he sees the past, the present, and the future and is weaving his purposes and plans in ways we cannot even fathom. We see only the back of the tapestry with its loose threads, ugly colors, and uneven patterns. He sees the finished product—the beauty of him working all things together "for the good of those who love him, who have been called according to his purpose" (Rom. 8:28).

Furthermore, we can't expect our past faithfulness to negate future sorrow, as if we have earned God's admiration and received a get-out-of-trial-free card. His love and favor are not earned. They're freely given. Past suffering doesn't mean we will be immune from suffering in the future. However, our past suffering can help us process pain, doubt, and fear with God when we allow it to so that our trust grows.

When the Israelites crossed the Jordan River, they were instructed to bring stones and pile them on the other side as an altar of remembrance for all God had done for them (Josh. 4:1–9). God knew they would forget how he had parted the waters for them. They would forget his provision. In the same way, we tend to forget. We need to look for God's hand in every situation. Our own "stones" are how we've personally experienced God's faithfulness or mercy. They are the ways we have seen God show up.

When my son had his seizure, the neurologist on call for the entire hospital was an expert on seizures, and she became his doctor for the next three years. This became a stone. The love of Christ was displayed through a brand-new church we had just begun attending and the love poured out on our family through cards, meals from complete strangers, and a gift basket of all the items our son loved. This was a stone. When we build an altar of stones, it's easier to remember God's care and faithfulness when the next hardship comes. The key is to reflect and remember. He keeps his promises and meets us in our doubts to bring us to a deeper faith in him.

As we begin to work through feelings of doubt, the best way to move toward faith is to acknowledge the doubt and remember the heart of God. What does Scripture say about his character? All throughout the Old Testament, we see how God kept his promises even when humans made serious mistakes.

When we're doubting, we also need that good friend, mentor, or counselor to remind us of God's character. It's always good to have one person we can call on who will speak the truth into the lies and share encouragement. In the middle of doubt, it's easy to forget and even easier to imagine all the worst-case scenarios. A reliable friend will remind us of God's love and faithfulness.

Recognize that doubt will come again, but now you have some tools to process those feelings. Focus on the ways you see God working during difficult times. Sometimes we miss them because God appears in small ways. When doubt creeps in, remember how faithful he is. You do not have to earn his love; you already have it, and he wants to reveal himself to you in your uncertainty.

For a special needs mom, doubt comes in many forms. We may doubt that we'll have the physical or emotional fortitude to make it through one more day. We may doubt that anyone understands us. Maybe we doubt that things will get better. We may even doubt that God hears us.

Doubt, in its simplest form, is confusion or uncertainty. After my (Sara's) son's diagnosis, I never doubted there was a God. I knew without a doubt that God existed. But I questioned what kind of God he was. Looking back, I never thought of God as cruel. Even after the diagnosis, I didn't believe he was necessarily doing this to my family. I still felt that our suffering on earth resulted from a fallen world, but I did wonder why God didn't stop it. Why was he allowing this to happen to my child? I couldn't reconcile the image I had of him in my mind with the confusion and hopelessness I was feeling at that moment. I thought, *Why is God so indifferent to my suffering?*

When our child suffers or struggles, it makes sense that we become confused. What is the point of their suffering? Will it ever get better? How will we adapt to this new life? Is it wrong that we doubt? Absolutely not. Doubting sparks critical thinking. Doubt makes us step back and evaluate the situation. We then can educate ourselves and come to an informed decision.

God wants you to know him. He wants you to trust him. God doesn't want an unsuspecting robot. He would have created us to blindly follow him without question if he did. He is a relational God who wants a relationship with you.

After I started doubting God's character, I finally asked myself why I was following him and raising my children to believe in a caring God. I felt like a hypocrite. Instead of giving up on God and keeping my children from him, I buried my nose in books and did serious research to learn about this side of God that I thought was simply indifferent. The more I tried to prove that God wasn't a loving God or, even worse, that he was indifferent, the more I came to see that he was even more forgiving, caring, and present than I ever realized. To my surprise, my doubting him only helped me prove my belief in his goodness. My doubt fortified my faith.

This life as a special needs mom is so hard at times—too hard to handle on our own. We need to rely on our belief in God's grace and mercy. We need to believe that this, our earthly existence, is not the end. I continue to experience time and time again that God's plans are so much bigger than I could have ever dreamed of or comprehended.

The most important thing I have come to realize on my faith journey is that my son is on loan to me. Our children are God's children, and he made them exactly the way he wanted. No matter what the world says, they are perfect. God has placed them with us to be their earthly guardians and caregivers. As much as we love our children, God loves them more. He isn't playing games with their lives or ours. He is caring for us and using this broken earth we temporarily call home for his glory and goodness. He also provides us with comfort and peace beyond our current comprehension.

When we lean into our doubts, we do the work of getting to know God. God's character speaks louder than our doubts. Knowing God's character doesn't mean we won't still have doubts. The difference is knowing God personally overcomes all of those doubts and insecurities; he meets us in our doubts. Go to God with your confusion and doubts (he knows you have them anyway, right?). Ask him to help provide answers or clarity. Go to him with all the mess; he'll be able to help you sort it out. That's his specialty.

Doubt is not the opposite of faith. Doubt can be a crucial part of fortifying your faith. Let doubt spark critical thinking. Begin to ask questions, talk with people who will help you find answers, and lean into the process. It's okay. God wants to be known. Doubting could very well be a crucial part of your process of forming a strong and abiding faith. The key is acknowledging that God is with us and he is good, even in those doubt-filled, sorrowful, confused moments.

Doubt can be a crucial part of fortifying your faith.

Psychologist and author David G. Benner writes, "It is relatively easy to meet God in moments of joy or bliss. In these situations, we correctly count ourselves blessed by God. The challenge is to believe that this is also true—and to know God's presence—in the midst of doubt, depression, anxiety, conflict or failure. But the God who is Immanuel is equally in those moments we would never choose as in those moments we would always gladly choose."[4]

Knowing that God did not judge my doubt but would meet me in my uncertainty was comforting. I didn't feel that I had to try to be someone I wasn't. We often think that we are "bad Christians" if we acknowledge the messy emotions surrounding our faith. As long as we are searching for the truth and expecting to have God's truth revealed to us, we will see God work within us and our circumstances.

God used my doubt and my confusion to fortify my faith. Now when doubt comes, I can hold on to the love, mercy, and truth he provided me in my darkest hours. I now know he is with me and he loves me. Always. There is no doubt about that.

How wonderful that even in our moments of doubt and confusion, when we feel that we are pushing God further away, he doesn't move. He is always with us and present in every aspect of our lives. It is up to us to continue seeking him, for he is right there encouraging our thoughts, guiding us in self-discovery, and providing the tools to fortify our faith.

Reflections

Jesus said to him, "If you can believe, all things are possible to him who believes." Immediately the father of the child cried out and said with tears, "Lord, I believe; help my unbelief!" (Mark 9:23–24 NKJV)

1. How can you give God your doubts? Can you take those doubts to God and remember that he sees you?

2. What questions do you have for God? How can your doubts help you lean into knowing him more fully?

3. Look back over your life as a special needs mom. Where can you see glimpses of God's beauty and purpose?

4. What are your stones of remembrance? How have you seen God working all things together for your good?

4

Comparison
to Contentment

Comparison is a game we will never win as mothers. Either we elevate ourselves to be better than others, or we look down on our performance and are filled with shame. Jealousy comes when we greatly desire another's seemingly easier life, and our hearts grow discontent and bitter over the reality of our own situations. But if we step back from the comparison trap long enough, we can see that no one has an easy life. Just because someone's struggles aren't obvious, like being in a wheelchair or needing any other type of medical device, this doesn't mean they have it easier than we do. They are bound to have their own challenges, but we just can't see them. All comparison does is make us focus on ourselves rather than on the amazing provision God supplies for us.

We recognize that life is hard, and it's easy to want what someone else has. Keeping our eyes on our own path is a daily struggle. However, this life is also full of beautiful gifts from the hand of God. He is holding these gifts, such as mercy, grace, love, strength, patience, wisdom, faith, and joy, in his open hands, waiting for us to accept them. We also know that our amazing kids display the image of God through how he has created them.

When we focus on what we do not have, we miss what God freely offers. As we move from comparison to contentment, we don't gloss over the difficult parts or have a naive attitude that everything in life is just peachy. We admit life is hard; sometimes it feels impossible. However, we spend a bit more time focusing on the good, and above all we center our attention on the One who desires to freely bestow his bounty on us.

One December I (Amy) was sitting by my Christmas tree, nestled in a chair under the glow of the twinkle lights. I could smell the pine scent of the tree as I sipped a peppermint hot chocolate. It was a rare moment of calm in our busy household, and I was relishing the sights and sounds of the season.

I noticed a stack of unopened Christmas cards and started to read them. The first card was from dear college friends. Their kids were growing up, approaching those significant milestones, college graduations and a wedding on the horizon. This holiday card also included a picture of the entire family on the slopes during a family ski trip. The next card depicted our friends on a cruise celebrating twenty years of marriage and photos of their children excelling at sports, attending the prom, and being surrounded by friends.

I love keeping up with friends, and I am pleased about their celebrations. I also know that one Christmas card doesn't tell the entire story of how a family might have struggled that year. But in the light of the Christmas tree, comparison started creeping in as I looked at those cards. At first, it was subtle. *It must be nice to take a ski trip . . . or a getaway to celebrate a wedding anniversary. It must be nice to have kids who don't struggle with learning and the pressures of adjusting to an Individual Education Plan (IEP).* As a special needs mom, I cannot do the activities these moms can do. They don't have the difficulties we have. The more I thought about it, the more discontent I became. What started as a joyful, quiet moment in a busy holiday season ended with me being unhappy, dissatisfied, and jealous. I was content until I took my eyes off my own life and started looking at the lives of others.

It is not just Christmas cards displaying happy families that can send us to a pity party. Weddings, impromptu coffee dates, having friends over, and the neighborhood pool party are all beautiful events we want to participate in. However, the mental gymnastics and logistics we must consider before taking our child somewhere can be overwhelming. We can never simply show up. We always have to be prepared. We are constantly adapting.

I always need to be on high alert with our child, constantly monitoring because she may act out or behave aggressively. Other parents need to check for wheelchair accessibility or bring food in case of an allergy. The list goes on and on. These are all situations that make special needs moms slightly jealous of those who seem to walk out the door with ease.

Sometimes comparison masks a more profound hurt. There are times when the invitations do not come or the wedding anniversary trip does not happen because we are home with a sick child. We experience sadness and jealousy when we look at the milestones our child may never be a part of or the empty nest we may not enjoy. It is hard not to be jealous of others who seem to have an easier life when life seems so challenging.

But can I tell you something? Jealousy has never positively served me. It always makes me look at my world and the cup I am holding as half empty. Comparison and jealousy also isolate me.

Jealousy is normal and understandable, but we have to resist letting it steal our joy and make us bitter. Jealousy causes me to walk through life with clenched fists. I do not want to go through life that way. When my hands are clenched, I feel tight, resentful, and sorry for myself. Jealousy colors all I see, and nothing looks good except what other people have.

So what do we do? We open our hands to God. Maybe we have to pry each finger open one at a time, but like buds opening up in the spring, our open hands receive the warmth we need to grow. We need to open up the places where we refuse to see God's provision.

When my hands are open, I can breathe, and I don't feel so cramped. I can look at life with joy and gratitude, trusting our good God. Gratitude is a daily practice. Sometimes it is an hourly practice.

Unclenching our fists and recognizing God's blessings are essential to contentment. The psalmist tells us that God has given us our portion and our cup, with secure, pleasant boundary lines (Ps. 16:5–6).

What is in your cup? Do the contents of your cup make you doubt the goodness of God in your life?

The contents in my cup are not so great at times—rejection, misunderstanding, and loneliness can come from parenting a child with behavioral issues. There are so many things to manage, like school, therapies, and medications. Many days I fail to see the good and find it hard to be thankful for the contents of my cup. To be honest, I do not want this cup some of the time.

When we focus on just the facts, the challenging circumstances in our lives, or the restrictions that come from being a special needs mom, we lose sight of the big picture. We forget the most authentic thing there is, that God is faithful, trustworthy, and loving. At the end of my life, I want to be able to say I lived my life with love and glorified God with the life he gave me. Yes, the contents of my cup may look the same at the end of my life. That would be difficult. But what truly matters is how I lived my life with what God gave me.

We can find contentment with the life God has given us, not a "grin and bear it" kind of contentment but a feeling of peace and rest that comes from our loving God, who gives us strength. We can see the beauty in this life he has given and purposed for us.

No matter where we are on our journey, one thing does not change: God is good. When we focus on this truth, we can say yes to whatever we find in our cup, the painful and the lovely. We can do this by allowing God to speak to us where we are right now. We need to ask him to show us the places where we fight growth and gratitude, the places where we see lack and failure. We can say yes to what is in our cup, the beautiful and the challenging, because our good God allowed it to be there. We can say yes to what is in our cup, the beautiful and the challenging, because our good God is with us.

I (Carrie) grew up the oldest of three daughters in a highly competitive family. We had challenges to see who could hold records in video games, finish a sudoku puzzle the fastest, or race a motorcycle the fastest around our yard. This competition carried over to extended family as well. My favorite memory growing up was seeing who would arrive first to my great-grandparents' house on Christmas Day. After a two-hour drive in several different cars, we would run to the front door and sing carols. Whoever stepped on the porch stoop first won! The downside is I carried this competitive spirit into my mothering journey. When my son with special needs came along, jealousy over others' seemingly easy lives settled in.

Comparison, competition, and jealousy among mothers have become such a part of life that sometimes we don't recognize them. When your child is diagnosed with delays or a life-altering disability, the need to be able to check off the boxes on milestone questionnaires begins to feel like the primary goal. It sometimes feels like a race to see whose child will reach certain milestones first. Whose child is holding their head up first? Who is smiling first? Who is rolling over, crawling, or walking first?

You meet another mom who has a child with a similar diagnosis. You become friends. Your friendship functions well for a while, but eventually, your child falls behind, and her child moves ahead. Suddenly, you experience jealousy, comparison, and, yes, grief, and the friendship falls apart. There are feelings of inadequacy no matter your child's diagnosis if (or when) they don't keep up with their peers.

The problem with comparison is that we feel like either a winner or a loser. We can be prideful because our child is doing better than others or full of shame and grief. After all, they're "behind." Comparing how our child is worse off often sinks us into despair. Instead of building friendships on common ground, we isolate ourselves due to grief, anger, and sadness.

How do we learn to release the feelings of jealousy and discontent? Acceptance of our situation and our child for who they are is first and foremost. The earlier we accept our child for who they are, the more we will notice the beautiful things about them. I'm not saying we never challenge our child to grow or schedule occupational, speech, or physical therapy. My son learned to eat by mouth because I had this gut feeling that he could do it. Many years later, he no longer has a feeding tube. However, I can also remember when I released my dream that my son would walk.

For several years, in physical therapy, he had been wearing bulky braces from his feet to his hips and using a walker to lift his entire body weight to move only a few inches forward. Outside of therapy, we didn't practice much because everything was so cumbersome. Eventually, we learned he needed surgery for scoliosis, and his orthopedic surgeon gently told me, "You have to let walking go." I cried because I believed his value depended on whether he walked or not.

Your child's value is not dependent on how they perform or what they do but rather on who they are—created as an image bearer of Christ. Your child will reach their own "inch stones," as Ellie Sanazaro says.[1] You have to pray for wisdom to know how much to push and what to let go of, and only you can decide what is suitable for your child and family.

Accepting our child doesn't mean we won't feel jealous again. Comparison is an ongoing battle, but it's best to compare our child with only our child. I love the phrase "Stay in your own lane." We sometimes miss how much our neuro-typical children grow in height until we're away from them because it's hard to notice things we live with daily. It's the same way with a special needs child. Begin to identify the ways your child progresses in their growth. Celebrate those "inch stones" and ask God to help you accept your situation.

Sometimes not only do we give worth to our child based on what they are accomplishing but we also wrap up our own identity in how healthy our child is or the obstacles they have overcome. The issue is that when our child isn't where we think they should be, we feel like we have failed. Our mothering is called into question, and shame and guilt plague us.

Our worth and value are not dependent on how well our child performs, grows, or changes. Our value is not dependent on our child's health, diagnosis, behavior, or whether they reach milestones or not. Our identity is based on being a person created in the image of God with gifts, abilities, and equipping. We have been called to this holy calling of a special needs mom, but we are a child of God first. We were perfectly chosen to be our child's mother, no matter how they joined our family. We are accepted, redeemed, and loved. Jesus thought so much of us that he died for us.

> **We have been called to this holy calling of a special needs mom, but we are a child of God first.**

When we accept Christ's work in our lives and know, not just in our heads but also in our hearts, that our identity is in Christ, we will care less about what others think and take steps toward contentment. We won't wonder if another family has it worse or better than we do because we accept that Christ is all we need no matter what. Paul, the writer of Philippians, tells us that he learned to be content in all circumstances and that we can progress toward that also. We can't do this in our strength, but we "can do all this through him who gives [us] strength" (Phil. 4:13). This is a continual growing process, and you can do it!

Don't let your ideas of motherhood success or failure determine your value. You are a loved, equipped child of God wonderfully and masterfully created in his image to display his glory. Ask God to show you your value and worth and to help you be content with who God created you to be. Your story matters, and you are his: chosen, holy, and beloved.

⁓

When my (Sara's) youngest son, TJ, was in grade school, I decided to take him shopping for clothes, which has never been an easy or enjoyable task. First, he is a young boy who wants to do almost anything else but shop. Second, since receiving his diagnosis, he has taken daily steroids, so he is much shorter than others his age. He cannot button his pants, since he struggles with fine motor skills. He also is extremely sensitive to fabric. Textures and tags are high on the list of things we must watch out for. Finding clothing he likes that is comfortable and sensory friendly, not to mention affordable, is extremely difficult. It's important to note that I don't like to shop either.

After what seemed like hours of complaining, sighing, and eye-rolling (TJ didn't have much fun either), we left the store. My son was still small enough for me to lift him into his car seat but heavy enough that I was not graceful in doing so. After he was situated, I went to lift his wheelchair into the back of the car. Our reliable vehicle had a hatchback that no longer would stay open on its own. As I kept the hatch propped open with my back, I tried to disassemble the wheelchair so it would fit.

As I rounded the car to the driver's side, I heard a familiar voice. It was a parent with children the same age as mine. She was talking on the phone as she walked to her car a couple rows over from where I was parked. She was talking about how excited she was for a girls' weekend away. She said she had to stop to buy a new purse for the weekend, but she would see them in a couple hours. As she climbed into her new luxury SUV, I heard a few muffled, excited "Woo-hoos!" She was in an adorable and trendy outfit, and I crouched down so as not to be seen with my hair in a messy bun and wearing no makeup, yoga pants, and a stained T-shirt.

I was jealous.

On that teary-eyed ride home, I contemplated why I was so upset. I couldn't have cared less about her vehicle. I'm fine as long as mine runs. I didn't care about her new outfit or fabulous boots either. No, I wouldn't turn down any of those things, and wanting to look cute or drive a nice vehicle isn't wrong. But those weren't the things I was truly upset about.

I was upset that my life was so hard. I thought, *Why can't one thing be easy?* I compared my entire life to that brief conversation I had overheard. I compared my reality to my illusion of her perfect one. That unfair comparison produced jealousy.

Later that evening, my little family of four sat down to play board games. As we laughed and enjoyed each other, I realized that jealousy had kept me focused on what we didn't have, not on what God had already provided. I immediately felt a wave of guilt over that jealousy—guilt that I wasn't giving my life enough credit and that I was jealous of what someone else had.

That's the thing with comparison; it rarely visits you alone. Comparison travels with friends like jealousy, anger, bitterness, and shame. In Galatians 5, jealousy is listed as one of the acts of the flesh or sinful human nature. I consider acts of the flesh to be both emotions and actions. When I feel caught up in negative emotions (any emotion that keeps me focused on myself and not God), I intentionally walk through an exercise that redirects my thoughts to God's faithfulness, goodness, and provisions. Perhaps these steps will help you too.

1. Redirect: Redirect your thoughts to what you know to be true—that God provides in all circumstances. What is at the root of your current emotion? What feelings or thoughts do you need to redirect back to Jesus, who is our one true source of comfort and contentment?

2. Gratitude: Intentionally look for things you can be grateful for—big or small. Write them down if it helps and spend time in a prayer of thankfulness for them. It is hard to be jealous when you constantly recognize the gifts God provides. Jealousy has no foothold where gratitude abounds.

   Jealousy has no foothold where gratitude abounds.

3. Mindfulness: Sometimes negative feelings don't go away swiftly. Give yourself time. Stay mindful of any underlying issues causing these emotions. Sometimes knowing the source is half the battle. What was leading up to this moment? Write out the time line of events. Sometimes seeing things in writing can help clarify why you feel a certain way. Or are these old or recurring feelings? If so, is there a time,

place, person, or thing that triggers these emotions? Staying mindful of jealousy doesn't mean you give it free rein. It means you are getting to its source so you can remove it from your life.

4. Share: Reach out and talk to a therapist or a trusted friend. Find a reliable and uplifting support group online or in person. Find a safe space to share your feelings. This step is the hardest. I don't know about you, but in the heat of negative emotions, the last thing I want to do is admit them out loud. But sometimes that's just what we need. Shedding light on jealousy destroys it. Jealousy, like all negative emotions, thrives in the shadows. It needs darkness. A good friend or a good therapist will help shine a light on your situation.

5. Remember the fruit: When I am feeling emotions like jealousy, anger, or fear, I intentionally focus on the fruit of the Spirit. Galatians 5:22–23 says, "But the fruit of the Spirit is love, joy, peace, forbearance, kindness, goodness, faithfulness, gentleness and self-control. Against such things there is no law."

Is jealousy, envy, or the green-eyed beast banging on your mama's heart right now? Choose a fruit of the Spirit and seek that fruit for one week. Let's say you choose joy; every day seek joy in Scripture, worship music, friendships, your family, working out, nature, or whatever works for you. It's hard to feel jealousy when your soul is overflowing with joyful blessings like your child's smile, a beautiful shade tree, a terrific book, a call with an old (or new) friend, or time in

Scripture when you know the Holy Spirit chose that day's passage just for you.

Jealousy in itself is not disastrous. We all feel negative emotions. If harnessed and used properly, those emotions can lead you to unfathomable gifts. Let Jesus redirect your jealousy to his kingdom work. There's no one better than our Lord and Savior to help bring you back into the light. He is the Light!

Reflections

I would have lost heart, unless I had believed
That I would see the goodness of the LORD
in the land of the living. (Ps. 27:13 NKJV)

1. Name one area of jealousy or comparison where you most struggle.
2. What is one way you see God's provision, goodness, or love in that area of struggle?
3. Where are you fighting gratitude and growth? Where do you see lack or failure? Write it down. Ask God to show you how he can fill your cup in those areas.
4. Write out a short prayer on a note card that you can tape to your mirror or carry in your purse that will redirect your focus when feelings of jealousy arise. For example, "God, I am very envious that my neighbor can just drop everything and go on vacation. Show me how your love is poured out for me today."

5

Guilt to Acceptance

The journey of a special needs mom is filled with many joys, sorrows, and responsibilities. As we juggle the needs of our special needs child and the rest of the family, this journey is often accompanied by guilt. Moms worry that they are not doing all they can to help their special needs child. They worry about their other children and their relationships. The list never ends. Guilt can wreak havoc on a mom who already feels overwhelmed.

Guilt can come with many voices, and all those voices can make us deaf to the One who calls us to trust and to give all our burdens to him. Guilt can make us feel like we are not enough. Whether it is an unmet expectation, a comment someone made, a moment of frustration, or a feeling we cannot voice, guilt is there. The condemning voice of guilt can make it hard for us to hear the accepting voice of love and forgiveness.

We can move from guilt to accepting God's grace as we remember the One who holds our lives in his loving hands. We can learn to give God our burdens and be free of guilt. Often, our feelings of guilt come from carrying loads we were never meant to carry. We can fix our eyes not on our shortcomings but on the Lord, who can lift the burden of guilt from our weary shoulders.

Years ago, I (Amy) was standing in a hospital as my four-year-old daughter had an MRI. I was worried sick about her. As I watched her small body in that huge machine, I felt helpless.

After what seemed like an eternity, the nurse turned to me and said, "Pick her up and hold her like she likes to be held, Mom." I stood there for a moment, confused. It was a simple request. Hold your child. But in that moment, I realized I had no idea how she liked to be held. What kind of mom doesn't know how her daughter likes to be held? I will never forget how shame and guilt immediately washed over me in a hot rush.

That was the moment when my mom-guilt went into overdrive. I did not know then that my daughter had reactive attachment disorder (RAD) and fetal alcohol spectrum disorder (FASD). It was just the beginning of years when guilt would hang over me like a heavy, oppressive cloak. And I would feel like all the challenging behaviors that come with her hidden disability were somehow my fault.

I am a mother to six children. I have had many opportunities to feel guilt. Mom-guilt is universal. We have this idea that we're supposed to be the perfect mom. We assume that we need to do it all and do it well. I think special needs moms are especially prone to this. But it is impossible for any mom to live up to this standard.

Feelings of guilt are often associated with expectations we put on ourselves. When we forget an appointment, lose our temper, or don't make it to a child's game, guilt rushes in. We struggle because we did not live up to the often ridiculously high expectations we put on ourselves.

We also let others' words have more weight than they should. In those moments, we forget to consider what God expects of us. He expects us to come to him and leave our burdens at his feet. He doesn't expect us to do it all.

How do we move past guilt and live a life of acceptance? First, we have to recognize the difference between guilt and shame. Brené Brown defines guilt as the feeling you have when you've done something wrong, while shame is feeling that *you* are something wrong.[1] Understanding this has been very beneficial to me. In my experience, most of the time I was experiencing mom-guilt, I was actually feeling shame. Shame can settle into our hearts and make us question our worth. I am learning that I need to change the story I am telling myself. How we tell our stories is important. Learning to reframe our narratives can help us move past mom-guilt.

When you experience a moment of mom-guilt, are you telling yourself the whole story, or are you looking at what happened in a less than gracious light? Seeing only the parts where you are less than and not the whole situation will breed shame.

Think back to a difficult moment when you held yourself in judgment and felt guilt. What was the situation? Do you recall how you responded? Did you find yourself being your own worst critic? Did you focus on only what you thought you did wrong? So often the story we tell ourselves is not, "I messed up, I feel guilty, I will apologize and move on." Most of the time our inner critic sounds more like shame, and the story we tell ourselves is, "I messed up, I am a bad mom, I can't get it right, I am not enough."

I relived difficult moments internally and was not always kind and gracious toward myself. I examined painful events with a magnifying glass, enlarging all the places where I thought I had failed. This kind of reflection is not life-giving. It leads you only further down the hole of shame and guilt. With God's help, we can tell a different story. We can look at a situation and examine it with grace-filled eyes. When I am reframing a story, I often ask these three questions:

1. What happened?
2. What story of guilt am I telling myself?
3. What do I know to be true?

I can think back on that day in the hospital when my daughter was having an MRI and reevaluate my story. I can look back and give myself grace. All I knew at that moment in the radiology department was that I couldn't remember how my daughter liked to be held. The truth was that I didn't know that my daughter had RAD and FASD.

I later learned that children with attachment disorder often do not like to be held. As a baby, she would hold herself away from me when I was holding her. I would come to understand much more about her disability as we walked the path of trying to figure out a diagnosis. I was at the beginning of my journey as a RAD mom.

The story I was telling myself was that I was a terrible mom, but in reality, I just didn't know all the facts. I needed to tell myself a different story. You can do this too; you can look back at a moment you felt shame and guilt and reframe the narrative. Maybe the story you have been telling yourself needs to be rewritten with grace and love. I believe that this practice can help us move past mom-guilt and shame to acceptance. If this is difficult to do, ask God to help you see the truth. You can tell him all that burdens you, every small detail.

The next time you feel guilt, how can you reframe your narrative and give yourself grace?

As special needs moms, we tend to feel guilty about many things. We're not doing enough therapy with our child. They don't have access to enough resources. But I (Carrie) want to talk about the guilt we feel when we imagine our lives without our special needs child. Maybe your child can leave home at some point or have another person care for them, but possibly you are facing the thought of never having an empty nest. You will be your child's sole caregiver for the rest of their life and maybe yours.

One of the worst times I felt the emotion of guilt was when I imagined my son being gone. He had gone into surgery, and I began to fear he wouldn't make it. My mind wandered through the what-if scenario of my son passing and all the feelings that would go with it. When I imagined the relief that I would feel—that he would no longer be suffering, that I would be free from the hospital visits, the surgeries, the cares, the concerns, that the trial would be lifted somehow—the guilt set in. Wait . . . what? How could I ever think that? How could I imagine relief and freedom if my son was gone? I would just be trading one type of grief for another.

Let's be honest; we have all walked through this scenario in our heads. We imagine if we speak the words out loud or even think them, God will wave his magic wand and say, "Well, you asked for it." We mentally begin pleading, "God, please, I didn't mean it. That's not what I meant." Then the guilt sets in for even thinking we need relief from this special needs journey and its many ups and downs. We feel guilt for needing a break. If you've had those thoughts or spoken those words out loud, be encouraged that nothing you can think or say will change the outcome of your child's life. Psalm 139:16 tells us, "Your eyes saw my unformed body; all the days ordained for me were written in your book before one of them came to be." You cannot speak a beginning or an end to your child's life. God holds the keys to life and death. He has written out the days for our child and for us.

Guilt, by definition, is "a feeling of responsibility or remorse for some offense, crime, wrong, whether real or imagined."[2] "Whether real or imagined" is the piece that packs a punch. Most of the time, our guilt results from taking responsibility for something that we cannot control, and when it doesn't happen, we feel guilty. As special needs mothers, we tend to feel responsible for everything and take on the responsibility that is only God's to bear. We cannot control everything. We cannot be everything to all people. We certainly cannot feel guilty for needing a break from caregiving. It's exhausting, and everyone needs a break. Leaving the responsibility for caring for everyone and everything in God's loving hands allows us a real place of rest.

So how do we do that? We have to understand the difference between accusation and conviction. The devil accuses us, and his accusations are harsh, slanderous, and full of lies.

Conviction is the voice of the Holy Spirit, which is kind, inviting us to repentance. Think of the parable Jesus told of the prodigal son in Luke. When the youngest son asks for his inheritance, it is as if he is telling his father that he wishes his father were dead. The son leaves and spends it on wild living. Finding himself destitute, starving, and dirty, he reasons that he would be better off as one of his father's servants instead of feeding pigs and eating their food. All that time, the father is searching for his son, and Luke tells us, "But while he was still a long way off, his father saw him and was filled with compassion for him; he ran to his son, threw his arms around him and kissed him" (15:20).

This is how God is with us. He does not accuse us but instead actively seeks our return. His offer of repentance is an open-arms invitation to redemption and renewal of a relationship with him. Jesus is inviting us with open arms to lay down our list of "shoulds," the to-do list we have given ourselves, and to ask him what he wants us to do. When we begin to see the difference between accusation and conviction, we can release the guilt of not measuring up to everyone else's expectations and allow God's Word to be our only measuring stick.

In addition, we need to live our lives from a place of dependence—not dependence on ourselves but dependence on God. Peter tells us, "His divine power has given us everything we need for a godly life through our knowledge of him who called us by his own glory and goodness" (2 Pet. 1:3). We have everything we need to be the parent our child needs. We have access to God's divine power. We have the wisdom to hear God's voice and turn away from the harsh accusations of the devil. We can live a life of godliness through God's strength. He abundantly gives us his wisdom without contempt or disdain because we've asked. He does not sit in heaven saying, "Oh dear, she's asking again. I don't want to give this to her." With open arms, he's begging us to ask. I know, Mama, it's hard to ask for help. But Matthew reminds us that our Father in heaven desires to give good things to those who ask him (7:11).

Ask him for freedom from the guilt. Ask him for the strength to be faithful in your role. Ask him for the wisdom you need to be the mother he wants you to be, and let this promise from James soak into your soul: "If any of you lacks wisdom, you should ask God, who gives generously to all without finding fault, and it will be given to you" (1:5). He does not find fault. He wants us to be free from the guilt we've taken upon ourselves for not living up to our expectations. After all, that's the very reason he came . . . for us to be free.

When my (Sara's) youngest son, TJ, was around eight years old, our family went out to eat at a local sandwich shop after church one Sunday. I told the boys to throw away their trash. I had a white sweater on, and after TJ threw his trash away, he came up to hug me. I saw the glowing cheesy fingertips coming at me as if in slow motion. It was instinctive to put my hands out and say "Stop!" and try to avoid the cheesy prints on my new white sweater. I was not quick enough. I did, however, mumble, "Great. Now I have to wash it again." TJ apologized for the hug. I told him not to worry about it but to wash his hands next time. I was irritated. I didn't give it much thought after that, though. I mean, what mom hasn't tried to avoid dirty prints at some point?

Later that day, I was in the laundry room sitting on the floor making my piles. As I got to the white load and put my sweater on the pile, I saw three perfect orange fingerprints. I sat right there in the laundry room and cried into that sweater. The tears were not for the sweater, of course. They were for those cheesy prints. I knew that one day I would be willing to give anything to see them again. Here I was facing a relatively new terminal diagnosis for my child, and I didn't appreciate a hug. One day every muscle in his body would cease working, including in those fingers that grabbed onto his mama and the arms that just wanted a hug.

Then I remembered the smile and the innocent giggle he gave as he ran over to me for that hug. He was proud that he had done what he was told and simply wanted a hug from his mom. Yes, I was worried about more dirty laundry.

I sat on that laundry room floor and bawled. I cried harder than I ever had before; I ugly cried. It didn't matter how much I told myself that my response was normal and that it did not reflect the depth of love I had for my child. I felt fear over the future, but the guilt was immense. I knew I would one day want and need a hug or an "I love you" that no longer was accessible to me.

The longer I allowed the guilt to fester, the quicker it morphed into shame. Knowing that there is a profound difference between guilt and shame has helped me on my parenting journey. Brené Brown defines shame as "the intensely painful feeling or experience of believing we are flawed and therefore unworthy of love and belonging."[3] Guilt can be productive, helping us match our actions to our values, whereas shame is destructive, enforcing our belief that we are flawed and unworthy.[4]

What started out as a moment of guilt that I could have used productively to remind myself that little boys always leave dirty fingerprints and to teach him that his hands need to be washed after eating—a learning experience for both a mom and a little boy—became a lie that I am unworthy.

I could have taken that moment and seen what a gift that lesson was. I could have said to myself that my reaction was expected but that next time I should focus on my child's action for what it is worth. Instead, I looked at my response, magnified it, and doubted the kind of mother I was. Not wanting to do extra laundry suddenly became me being a bad mom.

I believe guilt is something God uses to help us be better people. We are human, so we need a gentle nudge from time to time. We say or do something to hurt someone, we feel guilt, and (hopefully) we apologize or set it to rights. Because of this view, I gathered myself off the laundry room floor, went into my son's room, told him I needed to talk to him, and apologized. At first, he was confused, so I reminded him of when I was frustrated about the fingerprints. He began to apologize again, so I gently told him I did not respond well. I also said that it is important for him to be clean before and after meals. He apologized as well (mainly because he wanted to go back to playing). Was apologizing to my son necessary? Not for him, but it was for me. I needed to speak the words of guilt so I could let them go and move on.

If we don't let the guilt go, it morphs into shame. Shame's primary goal is to impede progress. I believe shame is something straight from the devil himself. God would never say we are flawed or unworthy of love. He sent his Son to die on a cross for us because he loved us so much. He loved us in our brokenness and sin.

I was diagnosed with major clinical depression, even before my son's diagnosis. I have found that shame is easily a companion of mine when I give it free rein. So I have to control shame, and doing so is a gift straight from Scripture.

When you feel shame, remember what God says about you. Remind yourself of God's love. He does not call you broken, unworthy, unlovable, or flawed. You can go straight to Scripture to be reminded of how God sees you.

- He calls you loved (John 3:16).
- He calls you delightful (Zeph. 3:17).
- He calls you friend (John 15:15).
- He calls you his (1 John 3:1).
- He calls you his workmanship—his art (Eph. 2:10, ESV).
- He calls you his heir—his princess (Rom. 8:17).
- He calls you bold and confident (Eph. 3:12).
- He calls you purposed (Jer. 29:11).
- He calls you wise, righteous, and sanctified (1 Cor. 1:30).
- He calls you triumphant (2 Cor. 2:14).
- He calls you forgiven (Eph. 1:7).
- He calls you blameless (Eph. 1:4).

Whatever guilt is plaguing your heart, give it to God. He doesn't think you deserve it. He wants to take it for you. In fact, Christ already has.

Another practice I use to move through guilt is to write down what guilt I am feeling. Then I pretend a good friend of mine is the one harboring that guilt instead of me. How would I respond to her? How would I comfort her? How would God want to comfort her? What truths from God can I share to combat the devil's lies? Many times, giving voice to guilt quickly eliminates it.

When we hold on to guilt, we are actually saying to God that his forgiveness is not enough. We insinuate that our guilt is more significant than his mercy, love, and truth. We are saying that his death on the cross surely can't cover our sins.

Let the truth of God's love be stronger than your guilt.

Reflections

I have loved you with an everlasting love;
I have drawn you with unfailing kindness. (Jer. 31:3)

1. Remember a moment you felt guilt and shame. How can you reframe that story through the eyes of grace and love?
2. What words of Scripture can you prayerfully meditate on when you feel guilt? (See page 79 for suggestions.) What does God say about you in those passages? Can you breathe those words into your weary soul?
3. What list of "shoulds" do you need to give to Jesus?
4. How are you speaking to yourself? Are the words you speak over yourself words of shame and guilt? How can you speak to yourself like a friend? How can you respond to yourself with love, comfort, and grace?

6

Anger to Comfort

As with all emotions, anger looks different for everyone. Anger can come in many forms: outbursts, withdrawal, controlling behaviors, defensiveness, anxiety. One universal aspect of anger, no matter how we express it, is that anger left unchecked can steal joy and rob us of comfort.

We may feel angry over the loss of control, the internal pressures to get everything done, or the unfairness of life. We don't want to admit we're angry. Often, we need to allow ourselves permission to feel the anger; it's okay to feel mad. It is a crucial step in not letting anger take control of our lives. However, we do not want anger to linger, as it tends to lead to bitterness or brokenness.

God wants to comfort us. He is not afraid or unwilling to meet us in this difficult emotion. We can take comfort knowing that even when we feel anger, God's Spirit isn't subjective to our emotions. God remains steady no matter our feelings.

Ultimately, God wants us to trust him enough that we can let go of our anger, giving it all over to him. He longs to be our most significant source of comfort.

One year we took the family to Chicago for a pre-Christmas weekend. We met with some of our adult kids, and I (Amy) was looking forward to having all of us together. I did everything that I thought would make this a successful trip for our child with reactive attachment disorder (RAD). He is very social, and I assumed he would love the activities. But the weekend did not go well. He was passive-aggressive and extremely oppositional.

As the weekend progressed, I was also getting irritated and angry. We spent a lot of money and time to make this weekend happen. His behavior made it a challenge, and it impacted the time I had with my other kids. I came home tired and crabby and, most of all, angry. I admit that I was upset at our son, but I was mostly mad at myself. I kept looking for the magic key that would make this child attach, and I had not found it. The pressure I put on myself to make this trip successful made me feel resentful, helpless, and angry.

I kept wondering, *What could I have done differently? How could I have changed the circumstances?* After our frustrating holiday trip, I asked our therapist these questions. She was not surprised at our son's behavior. She said that the big city was too overstimulating for him and that having our entire family together in one place was too overwhelming. Our son sees normal attachment relationships and cannot or does not know how to have them. She suggested strategies for a better weekend.

Unmet expectations, frustration with behavior challenges, and my inability to understand my son often cause me to feel anger. I am sure you have your own situations that cause anger too. Anger can rise up when we feel misunderstood or are upset at the situation we're in, the struggles our child has, or the insensitive comments of a friend. We can also feel angry that life isn't fair. There are just so many occasions for this emotion to creep in. The book of James tells us that we should be "quick to listen, slow to speak and slow to become angry" (1:19). I have always looked at this verse in James and thought it didn't apply to me. I'm a great listener, I am not loud, and I don't yell.

Sometimes anger looks like yelling, but for me it can look like withdrawal. Anger can creep in as I try my hardest to fix, solve, and figure out this life on my own or to control a situation. Running late? I get angry that I wasn't more organized. Kitchen a mess? I get angry and remind my children how busy I am and how no one helps. In the midst of difficult conversations, I quickly defend myself and justify my actions. Stressed about my child's behavior or fear of being judged? I am quick to be angry that others do not understand. All these scenarios may not cause me to yell, but they nurture frustration, and I'm suddenly unable to be quick to listen or slow to speak as anger wells up.

I have been a runner for years, but last year I found myself with a knee injury. I work out regularly, but all of a sudden I could not even walk a mile without pain. I went to a physical therapist and learned that my outer quadricep muscle was overdeveloped. It had done all the work, overpowering and overcompensating for my weaker inner thigh muscle. This led to a lot of pain. Over all those miles, my outer muscle was overgrowing and taking over. This caused my knee to hurt. I had to strengthen the weak muscles to put things back in balance.

It is the same with my soul. In the midst of the busyness and stress of being a special needs mom—the false narrative that I have to make our situation better and do it all, the constant worry and trying to figure out the diagnosis, the challenges my child has that are difficult—pride and anger have overgrown because they have gotten too much use in my life. Humility and comfort are weak and underused. In the end, it just equals pain—to my heart. Anger does not bring about God's purpose in my life or lead to comfort.

All this comes back to me not trusting God. How can we move from anger to comfort as we live our lives as special needs moms? We need to recognize that anger often masks another emotion, like fear or grief. We need to take this all to God and ask him to help us. With his loving help, we can strengthen our weaker muscles of humility and calm. We can learn to value the love and blessings in our lives instead of being bitter and angry about what is missing. If we believe and trust God, then nothing is truly missing in our lives. He promises to give us all we need (Ps. 23:1). We can stop cataloging our losses and look at the love in our lives. We can take everything to him who promises to never leave us nor forsake us (Deut. 31:6).

I become frustrated and angry, trying to change a situation that likely will not change. Yes, I want strategies to make our home positive for our children and family, but our home life may never be what I hoped it would be. Learning to accept our lives and the moments as they are is another way to move from anger to comfort.

We can take our tight grip off the idea of wanting our lives to change and just accept them as they are. This is not giving up. It is leaving our lives in God's hands, which is where they should have been all along. It is the way we come back into balance in our souls, allowing humility and acceptance and trust to grow. We can stand without the pain of anger and be comforted by God's love.

Two days before we planned to leave for a huge family vacation, I (Carrie) began to suspect that something was amiss with our son medically. It looked like he was brewing an infection, one common to his diagnosis. Usually, it is a quick fix with antibiotics. I was more uneasy this night because he was also running a fever. Hospital protocol recommended taking him to an emergency room to ensure he didn't have an infection in his blood.

The big trip couldn't be replicated. Several organizations we love and support were celebrating birthday milestones. Our family's favorite singing group, MercyMe, was a guest on the cruise ship. Taking a child with a ventilator out to sea for five days is no small feat, and neither is the one-thousand-mile driving trip to get there. We planned to leave Saturday morning to give us extra time to arrive on time for a Monday departure.

I had been doing laundry, packing, and checking off the endless to-do list when Toby began to run a fever and show signs of tachycardia (high heart rate). I hesitantly admitted a quick trip to the emergency room was warranted. (I see you laughing right now. ER trips are never quick!) He spent a few hours receiving intravenous antibiotics. Much to my horror,

I overheard the doctors discuss the dreaded A word: admission! They assured us he would be released on Saturday for an on-time departure. That night I got Toby settled into the hospital room. He looked and felt fine except for the high heart rate, and I went home to finish packing.

The following morning I received a disturbing phone call from my husband that threatened our well-laid plans. The new attending doctor disagreed with the emergency room doctors and refused to discharge him before Monday morning, the day our ship was scheduled to depart. I barely saw the highway as I furiously drove to our local children's hospital. I was so angry I couldn't think straight.

Whenever our plans don't go as expected, feelings of anger arise. As special needs moms, we want to rise and fight whenever we see injustice being done to our child. The Mama Bear comes bubbling up, and we would stop at nothing to help our child. We experience the adrenaline rush and the need to protect, advocate, and fight for what is needed or right in a certain situation.

Anger makes me cry. You might shut down, run, or lash out. When I arrived at the hospital, ready to have a long conversation with the attending doctor, who avoided me in the hallway, I ended up crying, ranting, raving, and venting to my husband about the unfairness of the situation. It was not a stellar moment for me. He had to calm me down. After my rant, I began to reason about fixing this problem. I called several doctors who knew our son, understood his body, and were willing to work with us to make this trip happen safely for Toby. I needed doctors to consider the upheaval for our family if we canceled the trip. This wasn't the first time our son's medical issues had ruined family plans, and I didn't want our kids to resent their brother. There was more at stake here than just a canceled trip—our family's mental, emotional, and spiritual health were at stake.

What do we do when feelings of anger arise, even when they are justified? Is anger always harmful? The Bible says, "'In your anger do not sin': Do not let the sun go down while you are still angry" (Eph. 4:26). Looking back on that hospital situation, I know anger was warranted. It's normal to have anger toward injustice, unfairness, and sin. I wish I would have reacted more calmly, especially in front of my son. However, anger is a normal emotion. Identifying the actual reason behind our anger is the first step toward comfort. In my situation, I was angry over the unmet expectation of a quick hospital release and the attending doctor refusing to individualize care and budge from hospital protocol that didn't necessarily apply in this instance. When you feel yourself getting angry, identify the cause.

Typically anger comes from the gap between what we expect to happen and what actually happens. These gaps warrant lament. Lament means pouring out our hearts to God. Being honest with him about our feelings draws us into the comfort he is willing to offer. In our anger, we have a choice. Are we ready to move toward God by identifying its reasons and releasing them to him through lament, or will we step away from him by allowing it to grow into bitterness, refusing his comfort? Lament and stepping toward God are acts of faith. They involve choosing to live where God has placed us instead of fighting him. Dealing with anger is learning to accept the moment for what it is, then allowing God's mercy to wash our anger away as we realize that this season will not last forever. Our current circumstances will change, so we breathe deeply, trusting that God always has a plan for the hard places in our lives.

We arrived on time for the ship after an early morning hospital discharge, a pharmacy stop, and driving straight to Georgia. Don't worry; our son was completely safe and healthy.

I learned a lot about myself from that situation, about identifying the root cause of anger and what to do with it. Anger is a normal emotion, and when it comes, we should learn from it. Recognize it as a tool to learn more about yourself and what makes you angry. Once you identify those triggers, then bring them before God through lament for comfort and peace. Allow your anger to motivate you to practice turning toward God. He's waiting with open arms and can handle all the messy emotions of mothering a child with special needs.

Allow your anger to motivate you to practice turning toward God.

I cringe at admitting this, but I (Sara) was angry at God after my son's diagnosis. No, I was livid. I was hurt. I was lost. I was that way for quite some time. I spent months postdiagnosis having what I now refer to as my quintessential spiritual temper tantrum. I put my Bible away in a drawer, not once ever bothering to open it. I deprogrammed my favorite Christian radio stations and removed all my favorite Christian playlists from every digital music app.

However, being a "good little Christian girl," I didn't give my anger free rein publicly. I still went to church, sang songs, and volunteered as needed. My anger was all mine, so I held it close to my heart. When I thought God was getting too close,

I would turn my back, grasping my anger to me tightly. I mistakenly thought my anger was protecting me. I was not going to be shocked again, and my anger deflected my vulnerability.

If I remained angry, sadness wouldn't destroy me. If I stayed angry, I somehow remained in control. If I remained angry, I would not be vulnerable again. No one or nothing would be able to surprise me because I was always prepared for the worst. What I projected on the outside did not match the inside. I was living a lie. When anyone lives a lie, the truth will eventually reveal itself.

The strangest and most beautiful thing happened when I gave myself permission to express my anger. When I finally said, "God, I am so angry, and I don't understand why you are allowing this!" he met me in that space. He was there. I even shared with him that I doubted him and just how sad that made me. I didn't realize it then, but I now know that, like any good father, he simply held me through all my emotions. He never held them against me; he merely wanted my trust. I was so broken, and I knew that if I was ever going to be made whole again, he would have to be the one to do it.

The anger was too heavy to carry any longer. I could not carry it and be the person I wanted to be. I didn't want to be an angry woman, wife, or mom. So I allowed God to work on my heart. I did not shy away from my confusion, doubt, or anger. I shared them with God and prayed for him to show me where I was wrong. He was waiting for me to come to him. God was waiting for my permission to work in my life.

It is humbling to know that our Lord and Savior, the Lord of all, the Alpha and the Omega, waits for our permission to enter our lives. It is equally humbling to know that he does not wait for us to clean up our hearts or purge all the mess before he starts to work in us. He wants us to come as we are and trust in him.

I remember crying out at God from the recesses of my soul. I have never been that lost or that scared of how I felt. I just knew I needed God or there was no hope. I remember wondering one night why even though I cried out, he never seemed to be angry with me.

Henri J. M. Nouwen said, "The movement of God's Spirit is very gentle, very soft—and hidden. It does not seek attention. But that movement is also very persistent, strong and deep. It changes our hearts radically."[1] God doesn't need gimmicks or diversionary tactics to make us aware of his presence. God doesn't yell; he quietly and persistently speaks straight to our hearts.

Psalm 34:15 says, "The eyes of the LORD are on the righteous, and his ears are attentive to their cry." I love this Scripture passage. In this verse, David is saying that those who truly honor God (even with their doubts, confusion, and questions) are seen, heard, and loved by God. God has his eyes upon us, and his ears are tuned to our needs. I find that incredibly comforting!

With his eyes set on me and his ears listening to my cries, God met me where I was, but it was ultimately up to me to let him in. I intentionally created space to hear what he had to say to my doubts, questions, anger, confusion, and fear. I intentionally created space by being in the Word, praying (not very eloquently either), and seeking the answers I desperately needed. It was painful, and it was not easy.

As I studied, I uncovered more than I could have ever imagined. The anger didn't go away on its own. The more I learned about God, the more I wanted to know. For every question or doubt I had, he had an answer. Honestly, there was usually another question or two to follow. He answered those as well.

Scripture spoke to me in ways it never had before. Passages that once were clever parables were applicable to my life specifically. During this time, I realized that it was okay to ask why, but the focus of that why changed. It was no longer "Why my child? Why is God allowing my child to suffer?" Instead, it shifted to "Why my child? What role is my son's life playing in the big scheme of things? My son's life has a purpose. What is it?"

Romans 8:28 says, "And we know that in all things God works for the good of those who love him, who have been called according to his purpose." It is important not to take this verse out of context. The apostle Paul was speaking to Christians. Paul was not discounting or even dismissing pain and suffering. He wasn't saying, "If you believe enough, things will be good." Paul was saying that as believers in Christ, we can find comfort in knowing that God will use our pain for a bigger purpose. Our pain will not be wasted. Our pain will not be for nothing. Paul was not saying that "good Christians" will not be afraid, sad, or even angry about their circumstances. He was saying that those of us "in Christ" can trust God to use our suffering for a bigger purpose—a purpose that far exceeds our limited view. Our pain, grief, waiting, and even anger here in this life have significance. We can take comfort in that.

Reflections

Be not quick in your spirit to become angry,
for anger lodges in the heart of fools. (Eccles. 7:9 ESV)

1. What is an unmet expectation that you can turn over to God today?

2. Is there an aspect of this journey that you desperately try to control? What is one small step you can take to release the pressure you have placed on yourself to handle a particular circumstance or situation and trust that God is in control?

3. Are you feeling angry and confused? Take a few moments to reflect on why you're angry. Ask God to help you identify the cause of your anger and to help you release all your messy emotions into his care.

4. Have you been asking God why? How can you reframe that question, letting go of the anger, leaning into peace, knowing that God has it all under control?

7

Despair to Joy

D espair can be dangerous. It can come on swiftly, exploding into our hearts and minds, or it can be a slow, creeping vine that suffocates our hope and joy. Despair can also be paralyzing, making us feel that we simply cannot get through another setback or struggle. Living with despair often feels like navigating absolute darkness without any light.

For mothers of those with disabilities or special needs, despair is a by-product of emotional, physical, and mental exhaustion. In the depths of desperation, joy doesn't seem to exist; at the very least, it feels out of our grasp. When the road ahead seems long, winding, and arduous, how do you fight feelings of despair?

With hope.

Hope does not mean that we pretend our lives aren't difficult, our circumstances are different, or the loss of dreams isn't heartbreaking. Hope means we choose to lean into God's love and grace. We choose hope even amid the hardships this life throws at us.

Despair produces darkness, but God is our Light of hope, leading to joy. The God of our salvation is bigger and more powerful than our most desperate circumstances, and that is reason enough to have joy.

Last year my (Amy's) child volunteered at a local nursing home. He made an excellent first impression, as he often does. I thought it would be a good fit, and he would be able to get out of the house and have some responsibility. I called the director and gave my standard spiel: his history of living in an orphanage for ten years, his sometimes poor choices, and his strengths. He went a few times and had some issues listening to adults, but they worked with him. I was not expecting to get a call from the nursing home on a peaceful spring afternoon letting me know he had been fired. My child was fired from a volunteer position at a nursing home for inappropriate behavior.

Immediately after that call, I was distraught. Instead of reaching out to God, asking him for grace and wisdom, I worried. I also got mad, felt shame, and went straight to the worst-case scenario mindset. I went on the internet to look for solutions. Then I called my husband, hoping he would make me feel better. Next, I opened my phone and bought something. When all of that failed, I ate too many cookies.

In a matter of minutes, I went from peaceful to stressed-out. I felt despair because this was not the first call I had received regarding my children's behavior. My husband and I have had many calls from principals and teachers. Our children have experienced several suspensions, and one of our children was expelled from the second grade.

It is so frustrating as I try my best to explain their behavior in light of the trauma they experienced as babies and the effect alcohol and drugs have had on their brains. With each call, I worry about their lives and futures and wonder, *Will things ever get better?*

Not once after the phone call from the nursing home did I stop, take a deep breath, and pray. When our brains are wrapped up in worst-case scenario thinking, it is easy to despair. Desperation makes us feel hopeless, like nothing will ever get better and our life as a special needs mom will always be difficult. Desperation steals our joy.

In times of desperation, I easily forget that God has everything in his hands. I fail to remember that I can ask for God's grace and mercy in every situation. I fail to remember that he is a God of hope and joy. I don't want his work in me to be undone by phone calls about bad behavior, complicated test results, or broken relationships. He has a plan, and my job is to rest and abide in him. This is hard to do. In every moment of every day, his grace and joy are available to me. They are there even when I don't ask for them. Often, I miss out on joy because I forget to focus on him.

Before we discuss how to move from desperation to joy, we need to understand what joy is and what it is not. Joy is not happiness. Joy is not an emotion that comes when things are going well and leaves when they are not. It is not a "buck up and smile and sing about the sun coming up tomorrow" feeling. It is not about plastering a smile on our faces over our despair. Instead, joy is a spiritual experience. It is a deep soul experience that we can have when we unite our souls with Christ, the true Light of the world who illuminates our path.

To experience this joy, first we have to remember that Jesus comes to us with a heart full of compassion. He weeps with us in our frustration and sadness. With his grace, we can let go of our desperation. We can cast all our cares on him (1 Pet. 5:7). To cast means to release, to throw away. Think of a fisherman casting his line far into the water; we can cast our problems away from us into the hands of Jesus, allowing us to step into his joy.

Second, we can find joy if we focus not on our circumstances but on God. Most of the time, joy eludes us because we want things to be different or we think our lives will never change. We focus on what we don't have or all the difficulties we face. We forget who is really in control. We need to let go of our desperate worry about the future and our expectations of how we think life should be. We need to remember that we are in God's hands and that we can trust him regardless of what is going on in our lives. On days I feel like I have no joy, I remember that his mercies are new every morning and that I can trust him. Lamentations tells us that when we feel desperate, we can have hope because of God's great love, mercy, and compassion. He is faithful (3:23–24). When we realize this, we can let ourselves be surprised by joy. We can recognize the beauty in small moments. Life may not be what we thought it would be, but we can see that life is precious and that there is beauty in the life we have. We don't have to stay desperate and hopeless, convinced that nothing will ever change, because God is always revealing, bringing life, and making all things new.

Finally, joy comes with the knowledge that God is always with us. Over the course of my life as a special needs mom, I have prayed so many desperate prayers begging God for help, to change our situation. I prayed for actual physical help: I prayed for answers and the right medications and doctors. It is so hard to pray with a heart that is breaking, when you feel hopeless and exhausted and you see no end in sight to the trouble and heartache ahead. I cannot tell you the theological reason why God allows suffering, but what I do know to be true is that he sees us, loves us, and stands beside us regardless of the outcome. There is no place I have been that he has not been with me. Wherever I will go, he will not leave me. This knowledge helps me handle the challenging, heartbreaking situations in my life that make me feel despair. Amid the suspensions, the phone calls, the isolation, the worry, I can live with the certainty that God is with me.

Are you suffering in a storm of desperation? When things go wrong, remember this: we are not alone—we exist in and through the love of God, and he works in our lives as a constant presence. We can find the peace that passes all understanding, which leads us to joy.

Have you ever been in the depths of despair? In *Anne of Green Gables*, the main character, Anne, tells her new guardian, Marilla, that she is in the depths of despair. Anne had been an orphan most of her life. Marilla had wanted to adopt a boy, and yet Anne had shown up instead. Marilla's cool reply is that she has never been in despair because to despair is to turn your back on God.[1] I'm not sure if Marilla is correct or not. Despair is defined as "losing hope, causing hopelessness."[2] Maybe in some ways she's right; when we lose all hope, we lose our faith that God can make things right again. Maybe, like Anne, we go through times when we can't imagine how things will get better. It's hard to envision how God will restore our joy when all we see is the darkness of our situation.

Hope is our longing for something more than we have. Think about the garden of Eden in its perfection before the fall. Our souls long for that perfection of connection, relationship, and beauty. Romans 8:24 says, "For in this hope we were saved. But hope that is seen is no hope at all. Who hopes for what they already have?" Hope is the tension between our unmet longings and our current circumstances improving. It's groaning through the aches and pain of this life with the desire that God will make everything perfect in the end. We know the earth groans under the weight of sin, and so do our bodies. We are eagerly waiting for "the redemption of our bodies" (Rom. 8:23). We are eagerly waiting for our restoration.

As special needs moms, we groan under the weight of our circumstances. Our lives are like a sine curve, with peaks and valleys, victories and defeats. Our hearts are broken when things do not go the way we expect. When that happens, we might react with cynicism. This is a self-protective mechanism.

Our son has had several hospitalizations throughout his lifetime and has experienced over sixty surgeries. In between these surgeries, my hopes would rise as I relaxed and life returned to normalcy. Unfortunately, we would head into another appointment, and another medical event would occur, requiring another surgery to fix it. Eventually, I learned to approach every doctor's appointment expecting things to go badly because then my heart wouldn't be crushed.

When things don't go the way we expect, another reaction is to ignore the problematic situation. We become unrealistic and act like everything is fine. Or we use denial to protect ourselves. It's been weeks, and we've watched our child have a reoccurring symptom. We're hoping it will go away. We desperately don't want to pick up the phone to call the doctor. That means upheaval to the calm. There have been times of peace when I thought I would break down if we ended up in the emergency room just one more time. I didn't seem to have the mental capacity to care anymore.

It's normal to want to protect ourselves from the pain of a broken heart. Our hearts break every time our kids go through something difficult. Parker Palmer says, "There are at least two ways to understand what it means to have our hearts broken. One is to imagine the heart, broken into shards and scattered about—a feeling most of us know and a fate we would like to avoid. The other is to imagine the heart broken open into a new capacity—a process that is not without pain but one that many of us would welcome."[3] We often protect ourselves from a broken heart when we don't understand that it is an opportunity for God to show up and open us up to new things—learning more about him, seeing small miracles, and experiencing joy even in the dark places.

Allowing God to move us from despair to joy means allowing him to use the broken pieces of our hearts for new possibilities. It means grieving the hard places, naming what is challenging and why, and taking our messy emotions to God. Yes, even our anger, reluctance, sorrow, and despair. Jesus felt them all. In the garden of Gethsemane, he prayed, "My Father, if it is possible, may this cup be taken from me. Yet not as I will, but as you will" (Matt. 26:39). I've often wondered how Jesus, who knew the future, prayed that prayer. He knew the cross was required as payment for sin, yet he still prayed that he didn't want to face it. He asked God to remove the cup if it was possible. He experienced the depths of these feelings for your sake and mine. His example shows us that we can take every grief and sorrow to our heavenly Father and be honest about their difficulty, even asking him for what might not be possible.

Instead of being cynical or in denial, let's learn to approach our despair with kindness, naming how we have lost hope and then taking steps forward, claiming the joy that belongs to us. How can we claim joy even in the darkest hours? By viewing our circumstances from a long-term perspective. This life isn't all there is, and even when things feel hopeless, we are *never* without hope. Joy can still be found. When you rewatch a movie you've previously viewed or reread a familiar book, the parts with tension are much easier to get through because you know the end of the story. The same is true about this life. We know the end of our stories. We know who wins—Jesus! So how do we survive? S. D. Smith writes, "We have to keep loving what's on the other side of this fight—the other side of this rescue—and that will have to make us brave."[4]

Joy is having confidence that God will eventually right all the wrongs and erase every pain. It's trusting him that complete restoration is coming, even when we don't see it on this side of heaven. We can have joy even in the darkest hour because the light of hope shines through.

We can have joy even in the darkest hour because the light of hope shines through.

"Not only that, but we rejoice in our sufferings, knowing that suffering produces endurance, and endurance produces character, and character produces hope, and hope does not put us to shame, because God's love has been poured into our hearts through the Holy

Spirit who has been given to us" (Rom. 5:3–5 ESV). Keep loving what is on the other side, and walk with Jesus in confidence, knowing that healing mentally, physically, emotionally, and spiritually is part of your rescue. It can occur in part even here on earth.

One summer my husband and I (Sara) decided to attend a conference for families, caregivers, and medical personnel impacted by our son's diagnosis. The conference was in Florida, so we decided to add on a small family vacation. One afternoon we decided to go to the beach and let the boys play in the ocean. This is where one of my all-time favorite pictures of the boys was taken. It is a picture of my boys lying in the surf, laughing with pure joy. I vividly remember taking this picture.

This picture doesn't show how the boys ended up in that position. The picture doesn't show that the walk from our hotel to the ocean took quite some time, since we went at TJ's pace. The picture doesn't show the helplessness that Craig and I felt as we watched our son struggle to walk in the sand even to reach the water. Every step was visibly difficult for him. His gait was awkward and strained. But he persisted, and he did so with a smile. As Craig and I were focused on watching him struggle and fighting our desire to pick him up and carry him (which TJ had already expressed he didn't want), TJ's wide, sparkling eyes never left the ocean that was before him. He was mesmerized. He was so eager to get to the water. You could see in his eyes that he knew something extraordinary was about to open up to him. It was unlike anything he'd ever seen, and he couldn't wait to experience it. TJ was so tired when he finally made it to the shoreline, but the expectation of what lay ahead was greater than his exhaustion.

The picture doesn't show that TJ's older brother walked by his side the entire time without any prompting. Being a typical healthy twelve-year-old boy, Connor bounded into the water. He went as far out as he could before I did the typical mom thing and told him that he was out far enough. Connor laughed and let the waves take him back and forth. He dove and laughed and enjoyed every aspect of the water. It was a joy to watch. It made me remember the first time I saw the ocean. It's a feeling you never forget. Such beauty holds such power, and being a part of it is breathtaking. I remember being so grateful at that moment that Connor was able to do the things I'd taken for granted my entire life.

TJ's experience, unfortunately, was much different physically. He was eight years old, and even though he could swim, he never went in farther than up to his knees. He would not let go of our hands. Either his father or I would walk with him, stand behind him, hold him up like you would with a one-year-old learning how to walk. We could tell he was terrified. I laid my hands on his chest and felt the rapid beat of his heart. His fear was palpable. But not more so than his fierce determination and his joy of experiencing something new and wonderful. He knew he couldn't stay standing on his own even in breaks up to his shins. He just doesn't have the muscle strength. His body doesn't allow him to easily do the things we take for granted. He would repeatedly say, "Mom, don't let me go." I would always reply, "I'll hold on as long as you want me to." (A more accurate statement I have never said. Ten years later, and I'm still holding on.)

Most people would be frustrated or upset by their limitations. TJ rarely has been. He never complained, and he never gave up or stopped that day. He laughed and smiled and enjoyed every minute for what it was—a new and exciting experience. But, as children will do, he eventually got bored with just standing in the water with his mom and dad and wanted to go back. Before I realized what was happening, Connor was lying down on the shoreline beside TJ. Connor showed TJ how he could lie on his belly and simply let the waves take him. Connor was never out of arm's reach of TJ. And TJ felt safe. Connor showed TJ how to let the waves work for him and not against him. Connor showed TJ how much fun the waves could be despite his lack of strength and stability. Did Connor understand the magnitude of what he was doing? No, he did not. That's the beauty of it in my opinion. He was only doing what Connor does best, making sure others are happy and included.

If you look at the picture long enough, I swear you can hear the joy and laughter and see the love between these two brothers. Their laughter was the kind that made everyone around laugh with them. They took what could have been a crushing, negative experience and cultivated joy instead. Connor doesn't even realize that by adapting this experience to TJ's abilities, he created a memory that the entire family can cherish forever. Our innocent twelve-year-old helped set a precedent for the whole family. Laugh. Laugh often. Laugh despite obstacles. Find the beauty and joy in any experience. And above all, see that God's power is all around us. Just like the power of the ocean, God's power holds such beauty; we just need to stop and let his power work for us and guide us.

Through the innocence of our twelve-year-old, I learned that we don't fight despair with our own power. To do so is futile. Instead, we understand that trials will come and that we will experience moments of despair. However, we can rest in the truth of God's promises. We can let God gently guide us to a place of joy, no matter our circumstances.

Duchenne muscular dystrophy blew our world apart, and up until that moment watching my boys play in the surf, I had spent months frantically grasping at pieces of our hopes and dreams, only to feel that it was like trying to gather the ocean's tide in my arms. I remember feeling utter despair, that feeling of utter hopelessness.

When I feel despair begin to crowd out my joy, when I simply do not understand why things are happening, I remember the story of Habakkuk and say, "Okay, God. I don't get it; yet I will choose joy and rejoice in you."

Habakkuk was a prophet. He witnessed injustices and knew more trials were coming. Habakkuk complained and questioned God. I believe Habakkuk felt despair. But even though he did not understand the why of what was happening, he trusted God's goodness and ultimately said, "Even though the fig trees have no blossoms, and there are no grapes on the vines; even though the olive crop fails, and the fields lie empty and barren; even though the flocks die in the fields, and the cattle barns are empty, yet I will rejoice in the LORD! I will be joyful in the God of my salvation!" (Hab. 3:17–18 NLT).

No figs, grapes, olives, or animals at this time was not just a stumbling block or a momentary setback. It meant a prolonged season of destitution, famine, and even death, which meant the absolute destruction of Judah. Even so, Habakkuk said, "Yet I will."

Habakkuk was not discounting the difficulties or injustices. He recognized them yet chose joy anyway. He helps me remember that no matter the ups and downs, the trials and triumphs, or the ebb and flow of this life, we can always rejoice in the God of our salvation. May we always choose joy.

Reflections

We are experiencing trouble on every side, but are not crushed; we are perplexed, but not driven to despair; we are persecuted, but not abandoned; we are knocked down, but not destroyed, always carrying around in our body the death of Jesus, so that the life of Jesus may also be made visible in our body. (2 Cor. 4:8–10 NET)

1. When you find yourself in a season, or even a circumstance, of despair, what are some of the initial ways you react?

2. Are you going through something right now (or continuously) that brings despair? Picture yourself releasing it into God's hands with confidence and trust.

3. How can you intentionally search for joy today? Ask God to open your heart and mind to his peace, which leads to joy.

4. Have you been discounting the difficulties or trials in your life, trying to force your despair into nonexistence? Don't minimize your pain. Instead, take a moment to acknowledge the hard places of your life, then say to God, "Yet I choose joy!"

8

Weariness to Rest

Ask any special needs mom how she is doing, and she will probably say she is tired. Being exhausted is a part of life as a special needs mom. The constant demands on our bodies, the sleepless nights, the hospital stays, the endless to-do lists, and the constant worry are overwhelming. The silent concern, the inability to slow down, and the burdens we carry that are not ours to bear can leave us not just physically tired but also soul weary.

It is understandable that special needs moms are exhausted, but this doesn't have to be a badge of honor or a constant condition. God calls us to rest. We can learn to give our worries and burdens to God and enter into true soul rest. The hospital visits, therapy appointments, and demands may not decrease, but we can learn to find rest as we release our lives and burdens to Jesus and lean into his all-sufficient grace on this special parenting journey.

On a beautiful spring day, I (Amy) was hiking with a friend when I got the call that my child was unresponsive at school. I was several miles away from my car. It seemed like it took me forever to get to her. This is not a call any mom wants to get, and my brain went into overdrive. She was rushed to the emergency room and then transferred to a children's hospital. As I sat by her bedside, I was overwhelmed by the constant flow of doctors and nurses, the tests, and the countless interruptions. Amid this activity, I made an extensive list because I was hosting a bridal shower, a graduation open house, and a birthday party in a few days. I am happy to say my child recovered and was discharged. Thanks to friends and family, the celebrations were a success.

After all the busyness of that weekend, I was exhausted, and my house was a mess. I had not slept. I had new appointments to make with doctors and therapists. I had to parent several kids. I was so done. I needed rest.

But I needed more than a nap. I needed quiet rest. I needed my strength restored. Did I rest?

Nope. I had so many tasks to accomplish that I felt I couldn't take the time to rest. Like I had done countless times before, I pushed through. I ignored what my body and soul needed, which never leads to anything positive. This was an intense season for us, but it wasn't the first and it won't be the last. As a special needs mom, I always seem to have many plates spinning at the same time. I feel like I am always in survival mode. At times, the circumstances of life whip me around. I am busy; my schedule is packed. There is always some big concern looming, whether it is finding the right doctor or advocating for help at school. There is the constant hypervigilance that comes with being a mom of kids with behavioral issues. I can get worn down by the continuous search for help and understanding and advocating for my child's invisible disability. I feel like a heavy blanket weighs me down. I lose perspective when I am weary: minor problems loom large, and everything seems catastrophic. I cannot seem to get the rest I so desperately crave.

In *Invitation to Solitude and Silence*, Ruth Haley Barton describes two kinds of tiredness. Good tiredness is what we experience after a job well done. It is an everyday kind of tiredness that can be overcome by rest and recovery. Dangerous fatigue is more profound and more serious. It can look like complete exhaustion. We are constantly in motion and always trying harder.[1] But trying harder never leads to rest; it just leads to burnout. I suspect most special needs moms are dangerously tired. I have found myself in this state of burnout more times than I can count.

This kind of tiredness is not fixed by a nap or a day at the spa (although if you need a nap, please take one!). This is a soul-deep weariness from carrying burdens we were never intended to take on alone.

Maybe you can relate. In the midst of all our spinning plates, why do we resist rest? Isaiah 30:15 says, "In repentance and rest is your salvation, in quietness and trust is your strength, but you would have none of it." Did you notice what the end of that verse says? You would have none of it. Why do we resist the rest that we clearly need? Why do we get to the point of being dangerously tired? Because as special needs moms, we think we have to do it all.

Can I let you in on a secret? No one will rest for you. You can hire a cleaning lady or have your groceries delivered, but no one can take a nap on your behalf.

When we stop to rest, we find peace and comfort. This relief from being world-weary comes only from Christ, but we need to trust to rest. Sometimes letting go of all we need to do requires a trust that seems impossible.

Matthew tells us that Jesus invites the weary and burdened (us!) to come and lay down their problems and rest (11:28). I love this passage, and I have read, pondered, and prayed this verse hundreds of times—longing for the rest and peace Jesus promises. But that rest seems to elude me.

The burdens we carry are not just the items on our to-do lists. Our packs become heavy because of grief, loneliness, or thinking we have to do it all. We burn out when we cannot trust Jesus to carry our load.

I had the assumption that if I handed over to Jesus my hurts, my burdens, my worries, my back-breaking concerns that had me bent over, Jesus would take them and hand them back fixed up and ready to go. I assumed he would solve all my problems. He does not promise that we will not have problems, pain, or hardship, but he does promise peace and rest. He asks us to take his yoke to learn from him.

Our rest comes from trusting God with our burdens. In learning to hand our heavy packs to God, we can also learn

Our rest comes from trusting God with our burdens.

to hold on to peace, to live in the moment, to have the grace to look for joy and gratitude. We will still be special needs moms and have many responsibilities. But we will not be walking alone.

So let me encourage you to rest. Rest is not selfish. Resting and taking care of yourself are soul care. Your soul finds rest in God alone, and that is the only place you will ever be satisfied.

Nothing can wear you out more than caring for your special needs child. Hospital stays are incredibly exhausting, and a mental topsy-turvy occurs when you don't know day from night. Special needs parents understand the deep mental, physical, and spiritual exhaustion from caregiver fatigue and the ongoing stress from the daily life-altering decisions that have to be made. Weariness is a part of the special needs journey that isn't often discussed. Life has moved on for others, but you're still at home caring for the one who will continue to have medical events or behavioral issues.

Compassion fatigue is common in special needs parents. *Merriam-Webster* defines it as "the physical and mental exhaustion and emotional withdrawal experienced by those who care for sick or traumatized people over an extended period of time."[2] Barb Stanley from Wonderful Works Ministry tells ministry workers how to protect themselves against compassion fatigue by doing four things: connecting to your mission, feeling valued by others, equipping yourself for work, and practicing self-care.[3] I (Carrie) believe this also applies to us as caregivers and can help us move from weariness to rest.

First of all, remember your mission. Your primary mission is to trust our capable God. Mental fatigue occurs when we try to tackle everything ourselves. Dealing with insurance companies has been the bane of my existence as a special needs mom. I struggle with living in tension, so I want the situation resolved quickly and painlessly. I worry about it and work to fix it. However, I have learned that my responsibility is to complete my tasks and leave the outcome in God's capable hands.

We have been led to believe that real life begins after we're on the other side of trauma or trials. "If I can just take a vacation . . ." or "If I can just get out of the hospital . . ." or "If the school would just fulfill their end of our child's IEP . . ." we say to ourselves. I'm not discounting the recovery that occurs when we take a vacation or aren't living in chaos, but we have to stop waiting for life to be calm to truly live. C. S. Lewis once said, "The great thing, if one can, is to stop regarding all the unpleasant things as interruptions of one's 'own' or 'real' life. The truth is of course, that what one calls the interruptions are precisely one's real life—the life God is sending one day by day; what one calls one's 'real life' is a phantom of one's own imagination."[4] Living in tension is real life. As my son nears adulthood, I have learned to let things go. I'm not saying we should never fight or advocate for something, but we should leave the results in the hands of God. He has our best interests at heart, and we will be less weary in mind and body if we trust God to resolve these situations.

Remembering our mission also means raising all our children to have a relationship with Jesus, however that looks for each child mentally. Once I reacted rather badly to cleaning up after a mistake my son made because he couldn't reach the floor. In my anger, I hurt him. It wasn't his fault that the accident occurred or that he couldn't help clean it up, even though he tried. I had to remember that if I continually act as if he's a burden, he will internalize that. I never want him to feel like he's a burden. I forget that my mission is not to accomplish a task but to rely on God for my strength and to treat my child as an image bearer of God.

The second way we guard against compassion fatigue is feeling valued by others. Now, this can be difficult. We're not always going to get a pat on the back for caring for our kids. Your spouse may not fulfill this need, or you may be a single parent. I believe we find our value in two places: our identity in Christ and our kingdom calling.

First of all, your value is in Christ, not how you perform as a caregiver. You are perfectly and wonderfully created just as you are. If you don't have people in your life affirming the image of Christ in you, ask God to give you those people. Also, try to stay off social media that doesn't feed your soul and encourage you. Surround yourself with people who will build you up, not tear you down.

Second, it's important for you to find your kingdom calling apart from being a caregiver. What is a kingdom calling? It's how God has uniquely designed you to display his glory and shine his light in the darkness in your part of the world. Your gifting might be watercolors, working with horses, music, or exercising. Just because it's not on display for others to see doesn't mean you're not reflecting God's glory. Any time we uniquely live out God's kingdom here on earth, we combat evil. I believe it also gives us a sense of purpose and fulfillment because we're doing what God created us to do.

For me, this is speaking and sitting on committees as a parent advisor at our local children's hospital. My goal is to make hospital stays better for other patients. Once a month I get to put on makeup, get dressed up, and not just be the caregiver at home. Every time I return home, I am energized. Find something that energizes you and do it. Ask God to show you. If you're in a season when even picking up an adult coloring book is too much, ask God for strength and affirmation, and be content right where you are.

The third way to guard against compassion fatigue is to equip yourself for the work. Prepare yourself for the work by connecting yourself to Jesus daily, as he is your best source of strength. This doesn't have to look like an hour of devotions in the early morning. Maybe it's listening to a podcast (like *Take Heart*), reading Scripture through an app, or journaling for five minutes. The length will vary each day depending on your season, but the goal is connecting with Jesus so you are equipped to face each day in his strength.

Lastly, we can combat compassion fatigue through self-care. I know this modern term is sometimes overused, but all work and no play will make Jill a dull girl. Once a mentor said to me that play is a form of spiritual warfare because, through play, we display faith, hope, and love. Think about that for a moment. Often, what is ingrained in our souls and minds is that we have to get all our work done before playing or caring for ourselves. But our work will never be complete.

Self-care is building margin and space in our calendars. It's taking time out of our day for rest and play. We often pack our schedules so tightly that we don't have time to eat well, exercise, or enjoy time with our families or God. When you look to schedule something else, look at your life and ask yourself, Is this essential? Knowing what you value and what is important to your family is a good place to start. Make a list of what is essential and nonessential and guard your calendar. Sometimes this even means saying no to therapies for your child. I'm not saying you should never pursue physical, occupational, or speech therapy, but consider your goals and the toll additional appointments will take on siblings and yourself. After my son got older, we stopped therapy. According to most evaluations, he's still developmentally behind, but it wasn't beneficial to me or him. It takes time to consider what is most important to you, but I guarantee it's worth it to give yourself space and time to rest.

Self-care is going to look different for all of us. What nourishes your soul may not nourish mine. One key is that self-care doesn't have to be a significant production. It doesn't have to be a day at the spa or an expensive massage. It can be a quiet bath, a fifteen-minute walk outside, some deep breathing, journaling, or whatever gives your soul rest and space to breathe. When you take the time for self-care, you're modeling to your kids that it's essential to take the time to rest. That is a gift for them and you.

If you're dealing with severe compassion fatigue or mental health issues, I implore you to get help. Needing a counselor, a therapist, or medication doesn't mean you've failed as a mom. It's also okay to say no. You will have seasons of giving and receiving, periods of plenty and want, and times of mourning and dancing. Live in your season, knowing that God allowed it for a specific reason and that you can trust him for strength and rest.

My youngest son and I (Sara) traveled every six months to the East Coast for nearly a decade. We live two hours away from the nearest airport, so we would drive to the airport the day before each appointment to fly out East. We would then spend two days at the hospital: day one was an infusion, and day two was spent at his appointments with the medical team. He would be seen by each of his specialists and be put through all the typical tests to help determine the progression of the disease.

The appointments always left me mentally and emotionally raw. What will the cardiologist say? How is my son's lung function? Has he experienced any more decrease? Every EKG had the potential to bring me to my knees. Seeing his heartbeat on a screen while I held his hand flooded me with emotions my heart didn't know how to name. Would I have to make a literal life-altering decision for our son with my husband on the phone or, worse, alone?

We had TJ in a clinical trial for almost two years. Every twenty-eight days, we would travel to the same hospital for an infusion and be gone twenty-four to thirty-six hours, including driving and flying. Our routine was so predictable and happened so often that we were on a first-name basis with the lovely woman at the Southwest Airlines ticket counter. More times than not, we knew the gate attendant, and even a few times we knew the flight attendants. We considered our hotel our home away from home for two years, and we had the hotel staff / pseudo family members to prove it.

It was essential to keep these trips as short as possible to avoid any more out-of-pocket expenses than what was necessary. Even more importantly, my older son and husband were at home. It was vital for our family to be together as much as possible. I wanted to see my oldest son's soccer games, dances, and significant life events. I wanted to be there for my entire family.

I was exhausted. Even more, the exhaustion had no end in sight. I became an expert at napping in the hospital and falling asleep before the plane took off. For several years, a weariness permeated every fiber of who I was. I wasn't about to complain, though. Our family was blessed to be able to take our son cross-country to be seen by some of the best doctors in their field. We had our son in clinical trials, and our family unit was stronger than ever.

I am a "grab the bull by the horns and wrestle it to the ground" kind of woman. I have always been strong-willed and persistent (ahem, stubborn). I am really good at powering through to get the job done, whatever that job is. But eventually, there is only so far I can go and only so much I can do on my own.

Then the clinical trial was canceled. We were saddened but also knew that the positive of this was that we were one step closer to knowing what didn't work as a treatment for this disease. Another bright side was that I would be around more for my older son and husband. I would be able to spend more time with friends and family. I remember trying to figure out what I could do with this "extra" time. I had been going on autopilot for so long that I didn't know how to rest. I was also constantly pushing through the negative thoughts, looking for the positive in each obstacle or circumstance in life. God had blessed us so much. Who was I to complain? Who was I to ask for more? Plus, what was it that I needed anyway?

Here's the thing with pushing through, though. Eventually, you run out of your own strength. There comes the point where you cannot push through on your power alone.

In all that time flying out East, I had not truly rested. I'm not talking about getting a solid eight hours of sleep either. I'm talking about soul rest, rest that can come only with giving your burden to God.

All of a sudden, I was bone weary. I had left tired behind years ago, was fully past exhaustion, and had settled into a weariness that permeated my entire being. My soul was weary.

My energy was depleted, and all I could do was ask God to help. I didn't know where he should even start, but I knew he would have to be the one to show me.

I honestly don't remember what I was doing. I just remember it was something mundane around the house. I either dropped something or something broke, that's all I remember, but it was enough to make me stop and say, "Okay, God. That's it! I'm done."

I could give you flowery words right now and say that we are never meant to live life alone, even though that's true. I won't sugarcoat our daily lives, though. Yes, God is with us. Yes, God has equipped us. I have no doubt about those truths. However, that does not make our daily lives less strenuous or exhausting—mentally, physically, and emotionally.

We know that setting aside what we do as caregivers, moms, wives, and servants of God is not possible. However, resting is vital for the ability to endure this life and its challenges. You have been called to this life, but that doesn't mean that God isn't calling you to rest.

Resting is vital for the ability to endure this life and its challenges. You have been called to this life, but that doesn't mean that God isn't calling you to rest.

When Jesus sent out the twelve disciples, he didn't sugarcoat their mission. The disciples would be met with opposition and physical, emotional, mental, and even spiritual exhaustion. When the twelve returned, Jesus immediately ordered them to rest. Jesus didn't casually recommend or suggest they rest; he gave them a gentle command. The first order of business was to rest.

Note that the disciples and Jesus weren't finished with their mission, nor were the disciples called to relax because they had checked everything off their to-do list. "So many people were coming and going that they did not even have a chance to eat" (Mark 6:31). Have you ever felt like that? You have done hard work only to get to the end of your day and everyone is still swarming, and you haven't even met your own basic needs.

Jesus is gently saying that this is not the way life is meant to be. You may be doing good work, but he adores you and commands you to care for yourself. Like Jesus did with the disciples, he commands you to go with him and find rest. And just like with his disciples, he does not expect you to get everything done (because that's not going to happen), nor does he want to see you collapse into rest (which very well may happen if you don't rest). No matter what is going on around you, he wants you to find rest with him.

Rest is not laziness, nor is it selfish. Rest is refueling your soul. Rest is creating space in your life to do the good work to which you were called. God's grace is sufficient for you. Embrace the grace he so freely offers and rest in him.

Reflections

Truly my soul finds rest in God;
my salvation comes from him. (Ps. 62:1)

1. Where are you pushing through on your own power? Ask God to help you let go and enter into soul rest.
2. What issues are causing you mental fatigue? Where do you need to let go of finding a solution?

3. What nourishes your soul and makes you light up? How can you find ways to play as a form of soul rest?

4. Can you recognize the difference between being "good" tired and "dangerously" tired? When are you resisting rest?

9

Fear to Trust

It would be easier to list the things special needs parents don't fear instead of what they do. That doesn't mean all fear is bad. Fear was instilled in every living creature as a survival mechanism. However, we can often begin to anticipate pain, so we find ourselves living in fear, waiting for the other shoe to drop.

If we remain hypervigilant about everything that might go wrong, always watching and waiting for what may hurt us or our loved ones, we will miss out on the blessings of today. We may also miss how God has already carried us through painful situations. Giving our fear free rein leaves no room for trust in God's master plan. Fear left unchecked and unevaluated can turn into chaos and mistrust.

Not giving in to fear is easier said than done, especially when we are faced with all life's unknowns and the realities of our child's diagnoses day in and day out. Learning to view those fears through the lens of grace, mercy, and God's eternal promises ultimately leads to rest. Trusting God in those overwhelming moments helps us not to live in fear but to rewrite our stories into those of triumph, resilience, peace, and truth.

Life as a special needs mom gives us many opportunities to feel fear. In my (Amy's) home, weekends were always tricky for us because we did not have the predictability of the school day's schedule. Our child did best when her day was scheduled.

One weekend was particularly rough. My husband was on a business trip, so I was taking care of the needs of our large family alone. Our child was being difficult. She was dysregulated and couldn't get her behavior under control, all the kids were home, and the weekend was busy. I was exhausted from the outbursts, so I decided to isolate her in her room to help her calm down and give us all a much-needed break.

With our daughter safely in her room, I sat down with the other kids to watch a movie. On this particular day, she quieted down, and I enjoyed the relative peace for a few moments. I assumed she had fallen asleep. After a bit, I went to check on her. When I opened her door, I found a broken screen and no child.

At first, I couldn't believe what I was seeing. I searched her room, but she wasn't there. I called for my other kids to start looking in the house. My panic was rising as I realized she had run away. We lived on a street that ended at a high bluff overlooking Lake Michigan and a busy road on the other side. I didn't know how long she had been gone or which direction she had gone.

The older kids and I fanned out in different directions and started looking. I was frantic. What if she was hit by a car? I was about to call the police when my oldest son, Davis, called to say he had found her. She had crossed the busy street and was in another neighborhood. My emotions were all over the place, my adrenaline was sky-high, and fear had overwhelmed me.

This moment caused me to fear, and rightly so. But this was just one moment in a life of many moments of fear; being a special needs mom has caused me to live on high alert.

Living on high alert makes you feel like you are trapped and cannot take a full breath. Something terrible could happen at any given moment, and that idea grows in your mind and takes root. It is an exhausting way to live.

I had a fear of tomorrow, next week, and ten years down the road. My daughter's behavior was so complex, and she hadn't even gone through puberty yet! I knew the statistics of kids with FASD and RAD. What kind of future did my child have? What if we couldn't afford the treatment? What if we couldn't find the right doctor? What were we going to do about summer? How could I do this another week?

My experience with living in fear has taught me that fear can quickly overtake our lives. It lies and distorts our thoughts and hijacks our reason. Fear can permeate everything. If we are afraid of one thing, anxiety and suspicion can creep into other areas. Fear and hypervigilance make us blind to all the good. Fear keeps us in the dark.

How do we learn to step out of the darkness and into the light? We need to keep our eyes fixed on the One who is the Light of the world.

I had to step down off my hypervigilance platform because it was detrimental to my family and to myself. It took me years to do this, and to be honest, I still hop back up there on occasion. I do not want to live my life with anxiety and worry steering the bus. Anxious living is not living.

I had to accept that I cannot change the diagnosis or the circumstances in my life as a special needs mom. But I can ask God to help me transform the atmosphere of fear in my heart and home. I can ask him to help me trust him.

I can meditate on the truth that he is good and his love never fails. Our ears need to be tuned to this truth. We need to get off the roller coaster of fear and take it all to him—the significant scary issues and the little, tiny fears we hold. We have to know the truth about who he is. One practical way to do this is to read the psalms that tell us about God's steadfast love and provision.

Fear is a prevalent emotion, but it doesn't have to be our constant companion.

This lesson of letting my hypervigilant guard down is a lesson I am still learning. I am on a journey, and God is with me. He carries me, leads me, is right next to me. Even when things do not make sense or seem particularly dark and foreboding, he never leaves me. He, alone, knows the way. I do not need to know (although I often want to). If there is a swift river ahead, I need to trust that he will get me through it, because he promises that the water will not sweep over me (Isa. 43:2).

Fear is a prevalent emotion, but it doesn't have to be our constant companion.

We need a peaceful inner place to stand. That peaceful sacred ground is with God. We cannot trust our hijacked brains to tell us the truth, but we can trust God to lead us into truth and peace. The truest thing about you is that you are God's beloved child. You can trust him. There is light in the darkness, and that light is Jesus. Walk toward the Light.

Have you ever felt like you've worn out your welcome with God, that he gets tired of you asking him for strength, courage, or energy? Several years ago, my (Carrie's) son's shunt (a device in the brain that drains excess fluid the brain produces) wasn't draining correctly, and his abdomen became enlarged. To ensure there wasn't an infection that could travel to his brain, we sat in the hospital for two weeks as he received antibiotics and had the fluid drained. By this time in our special needs journey, our son's surgery count was reaching the mid-forties, and at the end of those two weeks, he would require surgery again to put the shunt back inside his body. During that time, I struggled with fear over our son's survival. The fear seemed irrational. The current crisis wasn't that critical. He talked, laughed, ate, and got bored from sitting in a hospital bed. What was the source of my fear? When I began to explore the source, I found that my anxiety was rooted in the lie that we had finally worn God out, that he was tired of repeatedly healing our son after every surgery, every medical crisis.

Fear is often rooted in lies. I believed the lie that God was getting tired of me, our prayers, and healing our child. I forgot about who he is and the truth of his character. The truth is that God doesn't get tired. "Have you not heard? The LORD is the everlasting God, the Creator of the ends of the earth. He will not grow tired or weary, and his understanding no one can fathom" (Isa. 40:28). God understands your human heart and the difficulties of your circumstances. He doesn't grow weary of you coming to him. Jesus told the parable of the persistent widow because he wanted to show us how we should always pray and not give up. My favorite version says so we won't "lose heart" (Luke 18:1 ESV). God doesn't get tired of us coming to him with our problems. So don't lose heart; keep going to him in prayer.

Fear is also entrenched in the lie that we can control tomorrow. Jesus tells us in Matthew that we're not to worry about our lives, that even the birds of the air are taken care of, and that we have more value than they do. "Can any one of you by worrying add a single hour to your life?" (Matt. 6:27). Trusting God means leaving tomorrow in his hands, believing that he knows what we need and will provide it.

George Müller, who started several orphanages in Bristol, England, in the nineteenth century, was a man of great faith. He kept a daily journal of his requests and how God answered each one. He did not believe in fundraising for his orphanage but prayed daily for God to provide. One morning three hundred children sat down to eat, but there wasn't any food. George prayed and thanked God for what he would provide. Suddenly, there was a knock at the door. A baker couldn't sleep the night before and thought the orphanage would need bread, so he had gotten up at 2 a.m. and baked it for them. Just as the children enjoyed the bread, a milkman's cart broke down. He needed to lighten his load to fix the wheel, so he donated the milk to the children.[1] Maybe you require not daily bread but strength, sleep, soul rest, or a break. Ask him for what you need.

Fear can take root when we take our eyes off Jesus. My favorite story is when the disciples are in the storm, and Jesus walks on the water toward them. They think he is a ghost and cry out in fear. However, Peter calls to him and says, "If it's really you, call me out on the water." Jesus tells him to come, and Peter steps out of the boat. In the middle of a raging storm, Peter has the courage to climb out into the waves because he knows who Jesus is. He begins to sink only when he takes his eyes off Jesus and focuses on the storm around him (Matt. 14:26–31). One of the most significant ways to combat fear is to fall in love with Jesus and know who he truly is.

As he did with Peter, Jesus is reaching out his hand to pull us up out of the waves. He is asking us to come and take a step toward him in faith. He may not prevent the storms from coming, but he wants to walk through them with us. His peace is not of this world; it is divine. "Peace I leave with you; my peace I give you. I do not give to you as the world gives. Do not let your hearts be troubled and do not be afraid" (John 14:27). He is asking us to release our fears to him, gaze on him, and trust him. When we do, the peace of God that passes all understanding will guard our hearts and our minds (Phil. 4:6–7). Trust that he is near.

A friend of mine has a nondescript wooden cabinet on the wall in their living room. It holds an odd assortment of items: a fork, a name tag, a wooden angel with a broken wing, her son's first AFO (ankle-foot orthotic), and a half-used tube of toothpaste. It's their Ebenezer box, which is a box of remembrance. Each item represents something they learned through hardships, family experiences, and celebration. They take the items out and remember the stories behind them and what they learned about God because fear takes hold when we forget who God is. This idea of remembering comes from God instructing the children of Israel to choose twelve stones of remembrance after he parted the waters of the Jordan River so they could cross safely on dry land. Whether through a box, a journal, or photos, it's important to remember who God is—what his character is like and how he has carried us through difficult circumstances. Just like exercise builds muscle, remembering God's faithfulness builds our faith muscle so that the next time we face fear, we aren't paralyzed by it. Instead, our focus shifts from our circumstances to our faithful Father, and the fear fades away.

Nothing struck fear in me (Sara) more than hearing the doctor confirm our worst fears. We waited almost two months for an official diagnosis. We were given a couple different possible diagnoses, and I had done enough research to know what they could all mean for our son. Then the doctor confirmed our son had an incurable, terminal form of muscular dystrophy.

I grew up a Christian, so I have always been taught life after death for believers. I hadn't given death much weight. Sure, I had lost friends and loved ones over the years. But suddenly, I was facing something I feared more than death. I knew I was going to watch my child slowly deteriorate, lose independence, and suffer physically, if not emotionally and mentally.

I've talked before about the months after the diagnosis and how confused I was. I wanted to know why. Well-meaning people would say things like "God has a plan" or "God's at work." I knew they were right, but I wasn't feeling it at that moment. God didn't *seem* to be at work. God didn't *seem* to be planning anything. And if he was, why wait? Why allow the suffering? I just didn't get it.

This reminds me of the story of Lazarus's death and Jesus raising him from the dead. Lazarus and his sisters, Mary and

Martha, were friends of Jesus. In the Gospel of John, the story goes that Lazarus got sick. Martha and Mary knew how much Jesus loved them, so they sent word to Jesus, as he was in another city (about a day's travel away). But John 11:5–6 says, "Now Jesus loved Martha and her sister and Lazarus. So when he heard that Lazarus was sick, he stayed where he was two more days."

Um. Say what? As a friend, why didn't Jesus rush to Lazarus's side? Why didn't Jesus heal Lazarus from afar like when he healed the nobleman's son or the centurion's servant?

Not only did he not heal Lazarus from afar but he also waited two full days to begin his journey. So when Jesus reached their house, Lazarus had been dead for four days. When Jesus entered the village and was met by Mary, Jesus was "deeply moved" seeing her and the others' grief over Lazarus.

After Jesus asked to be taken to where Lazarus was buried, the Bible says that "Jesus wept" (John 11:35). He knew the outcome; he knew he would raise Lazarus from the dead. There was no fear in Jesus, but he still felt deep emotions.

The story of Lazarus's death and rising from the dead is fascinating. The short version is that Jesus waited not out of apathy but because of a bigger purpose. Some say that Jesus stayed where he was because, by the time the messenger reached him with word of Lazarus's illness, Jesus knew Lazarus had already died. According to Jewish belief, the soul didn't depart from a person's body for three days. After three days, the soul would depart, and the body would begin to decay. By waiting until the fourth day, Jesus was showing the glory of God. Jesus was demonstrating God's power over death.

Let's reread John 11:5–6. It says, "Now Jesus loved Martha and her sister and Lazarus. So when he heard that Lazarus was sick, he stayed where he was two more days." Did you get that? Jesus loved them, *so* he stayed where he was. Because Jesus loved them, he stayed two more days. What seemed like apathy or confusion to Mary and Martha was strategic for Jesus. His actions were bigger than Mary, Martha, or Lazarus.

We can learn several lessons from the story of Lazarus's death and resurrection.

- God is never late. God is actively working when we are waiting, perhaps even waiting in fear, agony, or despair. I pray daily for a cure for TJ. It may not happen in my lifetime, but I take comfort knowing it's not because God is late, procrastinating, or even distracted.

- God is in control even if we don't see him or feel him near. This special needs journey can feel lonely and isolating at times. It can feel fearful and out of control. That's when I need to take a deep breath and remember that God's got this. He is in control—*actively* in control.

- God cares. Even as he is working everything out for his glory and our good, he feels our pain. Jesus wept when he saw the people mourning and was saddened by Lazarus's death. That wasn't the only time either. After John the Baptist was killed, Jesus removed himself from the crowds to be alone and mourn. God's love is not a detached love. His love is authentic and active. Our feelings are valid. He wants us to turn to him with those feelings and let him work through them.

As special needs moms, our fears are deep, and they are vast. We deal with medical, mental, emotional, financial, behavioral issues . . . the list goes on. What happens, then, when fear is here to stay? How do we live *with* fear but not live *in* fear?

When fear seems to be permeating every aspect of my life, I do a Facts over Fear exercise.

1. **Grace to feel.** I write down exactly what I'm feeling. I don't hold back, and I don't judge myself. I tell myself my feelings are okay and normal. They are an initial response to a genuine threat. I sit in the space and allow myself to feel all the feels.

2. **Just the facts.** I underline or highlight the facts in what I just wrote down—just the facts as a judge would see them. I then cross out the rest—even if it contains valid fears. Ultimately, I just want to see the facts. (No could-haves, should-haves, or shouldn't-haves are allowed here.)

3. **Promises and protection.** If what remains is still fearful and overwhelming, I write one of God's promises next to it, the name of someone who is currently in my corner, or how I'm now doing my best to protect myself and/or my loved ones from the danger.

4. **Rewrite the story.** I rewrite the fear as it now stands as fact. Rewrite the original story but only what was highlighted, leaving out everything that was crossed off.

This exercise doesn't eliminate the fear or keep it from returning. It's not meant to invalidate our fear. Our fear is genuine. However, I find comfort knowing I have the power to rewrite my fear into something strong and courageous in the moment. Or, at the very least, I can find comfort in the fact that my faith is bigger than my fear.

Ultimately, I *experience* fear, but I don't live *for* it, and my family doesn't live *in* it.

We have not been promised an easy life here on earth. It's a broken world we live in. But God has promised us that he will help us overcome it. The power we have in Christ can rewrite our stories.

Reflections

But now, this is what the LORD says—
   he who created you, Jacob,
   he who formed you, Israel:
"Do not fear, for I have redeemed you;
   I have summoned you by name; you are mine."
   (Isa. 43:1)

1. What recurring fear do you have? Take a moment to pray, asking God to remove that fear and to help you trust in his love for you.

2. How would it feel to release your fear to God? Would your body relax? Would your breath come easier? Picture yourself releasing the tight grip you have on fear, holding your hands out to God, asking and trusting him to take it. Rest in the freedom that only faithfulness can bring.

3. Releasing fear and trusting God take practice. For the next few days, intentionally exercise your faith muscle.

Close your eyes, breathe out your worries, and breathe in God's truth. Repeat as needed.

4. How would focusing on God's truth instead of the lies we believe help you release the grip fear holds on your mama's heart?

10

Overwhelm
to Relinquishment

S pecial needs mothers fill several roles in their children's lives: nurse, facilitator, advocate, caregiver, psychologist, physician, teacher, nutritionist, intervention specialist, and therapist, just to name a few. We manage various parts of our children's lives, and they greatly depend on us. As a result, we are often overwhelmed and believe that everything relies on us. We have to be in control because, after all, it's our job.

Relinquishing control is an area in which most humans struggle. Yet, God invites us to release our tight grasp on our children. Our children are only on loan to us, and we mistakenly believe that we can determine the outcome of their lives. Relinquishing control is a deliberate choice to trust God's sovereignty, to daily release our children to him and the perfect plan he has for their lives and ours. We know this isn't easy, but it comes with changing our mindset. When we surrender control, we are stepping into freedom because we can perform our duties with the perfect power of the Holy Spirit. This doesn't mean we are quitting. Rather, we are faithfully mothering our children with a burden lifted because the outcome doesn't depend on us. We have made a deliberate choice to rely on God's strength and to trust his sovereignty.

⁓

I (Amy) was standing in line at the store when I felt my phone buzz. I looked down, and my heart sank. The principal was calling, again. Our son was exhibiting some challenging behaviors, and I needed to pick him up. This was obviously not on my agenda for the day.

We were in the middle of moving, had one house on the market, and were renovating another. I had boxes everywhere and couldn't find anything. We were also in the process of finding our daughter a new residential boarding school. So when I wasn't packing boxes, I was filling out applications and making phone calls. This whole period of time was stressful. I was overwhelmed, tired of holding it all together, and burned out. I felt like I could never get anything done, let alone savor life. I wanted to quit.

As I was driving to pick up my child (with a less than positive attitude), I noticed the beauty of the autumn leaves in their final burst of color before falling to the ground. They were beautiful in their last breath of life. I was reminded that Jesus said we must fall to the ground and die to bear fruit (John 12:24). Dying is essential for a new life. It is incredibly painful, but there is beauty in it if we have the eyes to see. I have to die to my tightfisted ways in order to experience beauty and new life. I have to trust the Giver of life to bring new life to me and my situation. So often I stop trusting him and put my trust in myself. That leads to me feeling continually overwhelmed.

Often when I am feeling overwhelmed, it is because I'm trying too hard to control a situation. I'm trying to call all the shots. I know that God has a plan, but I have ten more that I think are better. I have the misguided notion that I am in control.

There are so many aspects of our lives as special needs moms that are not what we expected. We are asked daily to surrender our own will, plans, and ideas for the sake of those we care for. We often miss the gift and beauty of the moment because we are trying so hard to control our lives. For me to relinquish my control, something has to give. I have to give up choosing my own way.

I need a shift in my perspective, and I need to widen my view. When I look at something too closely, I lose perspective. I see only the problems and scarcity. When I focus on only the problems in front of me, I forget to bring them to God. I forget that God is faithful even in the midst of moving boxes, challenging behaviors, medical appointments, and my ever growing to-do list. Changing my perspective reminds me that I do not control the outcome. Each new situation gives me the opportunity to surrender the outcome to God and to discover something new about my life, our God, and my children. Surrendering to God is how we walk this path as special needs moms with peace and joy.

Surrendering the outcome to God is not easy. In fact, it's completely counterintuitive to how we usually live our lives as special needs moms. We are always in problem-solving mode, a necessity as we make decisions and find solutions to help our children. I often assume that I will regain peace if I can solve the problem at hand.

But what if we looked for peace first? Instead of running off in all directions looking for answers to our anxiety-producing problems, what if we stopped and were quiet and prayed? What if we chose to surrender the moment before we looked for answers?

Surrender does not mean giving up. It means placing our burdens in the capable hands of our loving Father. We can surrender because we recognize God's faithfulness and goodness.

We need to bring everything to him, all of it. No matter how big or small. We don't get to decide how and when he will fix it. We just need to bring it and lay it down at his feet. He supplies exactly what we need every single time.

Surrendering to God helps us to be fully present and grateful in the moment. We may not get to choose our circumstances, but we can choose how present we are, how obedient, how joyful. We can let go of our need to solve every problem and let the gift of his life and beauty overwhelm us.

Changing our perspective reminds us that every single aspect of our lives has the imprint of God's love, provision, and faithfulness.

Changing our perspective reminds us that every single aspect of our lives has the imprint of God's love, provision, and faithfulness. When we surrender to God, it opens our eyes to the abundance of our good God. When we look at our lives in the frame of his abundance, we can trust him each step of the way. We can trust him to guide us in our parenting, we can rely on him to bring about his good will for our children, we can remember that his loving goodness and care will sustain us even in the midst of the most challenging day.

When I give my overwhelmed heart to God, I am reminded that being a special needs mom can be messy, frantic, and busy, but it is also beautiful. Relinquishment helps us to see the joys of the journey. His love for us never fails, and he holds everything in his hands.

I (Carrie) am the oldest of three girls and a typical type A firstborn. I was constantly bossing my two younger sisters around, and the roles of teacher and mom were the only ones I would claim during pretend play. I would be pretty wealthy if I had a dime for the frequent times I heard, "Carrie, I'm the mom; you're not." These tendencies haven't gone away as I've aged. I still have this incredible desire to be in control. Ask my husband about the early days of our marriage and arguments regarding his driving. Thankfully, after twenty-plus years of marriage, I have learned to hold my tongue (or maybe he's a fine driver after all).

As moms, we experience being out of control. Whether our child had a prenatal diagnosis, was diagnosed later in life, or has hidden mental or behavioral disabilities, we have little say in the outcome. We don't get a vote on what will come our way, what type of medical care our child may require, or our child's behavior. At times, this lack of control prompts us to overcompensate in the areas we think we can control: our schedules, our other children, our husbands. When it comes to the day-to-day decisions and planning, I step back and tell God, "I've got this; just watch me work." Can you relate?

I've often been overwhelmed with the desire to control outcomes and make things fair and even for our other three children. Toby has two older brothers, relatively close to his age, and one younger sister. Early on, I resolved that Toby's medical issues wouldn't become a point of resentment for our other children. Both sets of grandparents were often called upon to stay with them during extended hospital stays or doctor appointments. Trying to achieve fairness in families is like chasing the wind. It will never be caught. The important thing here is relinquishment of control. We cannot shield our children from their sibling's needs, but they should also know that their needs and feelings are valid. The time we spend with each of our children isn't going to be equal, and we're not going to be perfect parents. God isn't asking for perfection; he's asking for our faithfulness. God can take our meager offerings and create something beautiful. He created Adam out of the dust, he fed the five thousand with a child's small lunch, and Goliath was taken down with a small stone. God is in the small. Let's relinquish control and be faithful with what he's given us.

The first step to relinquishment is acknowledging and accepting that we aren't in control. The truth is that I can't make up for even a tiny portion of the ways that our son's medical needs have affected our family, but I can model to my children how to react when life doesn't go as expected. We do have autonomy over our attitudes. It's a natural desire to protect ourselves and other family members from pain, but it's a futile endeavor when this is always our goal.

The next step to surrender is allowing our hearts to trust that God loves us and wants what is best for us. Acknowledging in our heads that this is true is easy, but it's more difficult for our hearts to accept that he genuinely loves all of us—even our sinful, broken pieces.

"How precious to me are your thoughts, God! How vast is the sum of them! Were I to count them, they would outnumber the grains of sand" (Ps. 139:17–18). If you've ever walked on a beach, you know that it would be futile to try to count the grains in a shovel full of sand, let alone an entire beach. Multiply that by the number of beaches globally, and the number of grains stretches into eternity. God's thoughts are precious. When we begin to trust his great love for us, we understand that even our trials have been sifted through the hands of a loving heavenly Father.

Lastly, we need to turn all our plans over to God, even the small ones. Proverbs 16:3 urges us to "commit to the LORD whatever you do, and he will establish your plans." Instead of asking God to bless your day, ask him for the day's plans. When my husband and I were expecting our first baby, I would go shopping at Babies R Us and admire the matching nursery furniture: the crib, rocking chair, changing table, and dresser. I would have loved to have them, but they were out of our price range, so I gave up that expectation. Then the Holy Spirit nudged me to begin praying for matching furniture. After several months, my mom found a crib, changing table, and rocker at a garage sale. They weren't Babies R Us new, but they were beautiful and coordinated. God cares for your needs and even your wants. Relinquishment is an invitation to allow God to show you how he cares about every part of your life.

Releasing control removes the burden from our shoulders and the responsibility for our child's mental, emotional, and spiritual well-being. We research treatments and discuss with other parents online, struggling to figure everything out independently. We act as if one wrong decision will mess up our child forever. This is not a burden we need to bear. Relinquishment often looks like doing nothing or being patient.

I struggle with living in tension. I want all my problems to be solved quickly. Sometimes, though, I'm so quick to fix a problem when a solution would have presented itself easily if I had just waited. It's like clicking the Complete Order button on an online shopping site only to realize you need one more thing. But it's too late; you'll have to pay for shipping again to order the one thing you missed. Relinquishment is an invitation from God to lighten our load and our burdens and let him do the figuring, mental gymnastics, and purposing of our child's life.

Learning to give up control is a daily practice of releasing the tight grip on our lives and assuming the posture of open hands and palms lifted, waiting to receive what God has, waiting to hear his plans for us. The ways he orchestrates his methods are more impressive than we can imagine. There is freedom from overwhelm in relinquishing our lives to our heavenly Father.

Control is a touchy subject for me (Sara). It is something I have struggled with and will have to work on my entire life.

Relinquishing or surrendering control means trusting the sovereignty, or supreme power, of our Lord and Savior. It means letting go. It means trusting God's plan more than our limited view of what we thought our plan here on earth should be.

Surrendering to God's plan, or relinquishing our limited view of what our lives should look like, does not mean we quit or give up on our child with special needs. Relinquishing control does not mean we stop fighting for our child's rights, better medical care, fair treatment at school, and accessibility. It doesn't mean we stop advocating for our child.

Surrendering to God's plan does not require us to be okay with our child's diagnosis. My son is happy, and he loves life. That does not mean he doesn't get frustrated or wish he was pain-free or had it a little easier. As a mom, watching him struggle can be difficult. Yes, it can bring me to tears at times. However, I know God has a plan for my son. God's plan for our child is not contingent on our ability to understand or agree.

When we think of surrendering or relinquishing control, we think of losing and being forced to surrender and submit to another entity or power. In our worldview, that's a negative consequence of surrendering. It's often accompanied by a forced change we don't want. In God's eternal view, surrendering does mean submitting to God's higher power. The difference is that when we surrender to him, we acknowledge and accept that he sent his Son to earth to die for our sins. We aren't surrendering because we are losing a battle. The battle has already been won! Surrendering means we accept the peace that follows that battle with the assurance that we are on the winning side.

Our surrendering to God isn't without action on our part. Surrendering is not quitting. Quitting is a cease in action. Quitting means we stop doing whatever we're doing—productive or not. Surrendering is an action. It is a choice we make in a pivotal moment of our lives.

I'm a visual person, so quitting to me looks like giving up and letting go of whatever we had a death grip on, whatever we were grasping by the tips of our fingers. Relinquishing means holding our hands out, palms up, letting God take from us what we were not meant to carry. It is understanding that we have to let go of something in order to receive something good from God.

One of my favorite Scripture passages is Psalm 46:10: "Be still, and know I am God." It means "Stop!" or "Cease!" or "I am God. Girl, relax!" (Okay, so the last part isn't an official translation, but it is still relevant.) Giving up control means sitting in peace with what God has in store. It doesn't mean we won't have questions or we won't have bad days. The verse also doesn't say that a good Christian will always be still and know that he is God. There's a reason why it says, "Stop! Trust that I am God." He knows we need that reminder. After my son's diagnosis, a friend sent a necklace with this Scripture passage on a charm. I spent the first few years rubbing that charm until I could no longer see the verse. It was a practical way I could remind myself to relax, acknowledge God's control over my life, and surrender to his way of grace, love, and mercy.

Another wonderful verse I refer to often is Matthew 6:34, which says, "Therefore do not worry about tomorrow, for tomorrow will worry about itself. Each day has enough trouble of its own." I love this verse because it doesn't sugarcoat life. It doesn't say we shouldn't worry because we should know that God has everything under control. Nowhere does it say, "Don't worry about tomorrow because everything is gonna be great." No, it acknowledges the worry. It acknowledges that life is complex and that we all have trouble. Life will have difficulties and heartache, but when we know the perfect outcome through Jesus Christ, we can settle into the joy of today—no matter the circumstances.

I would be lying if I said I don't worry. I do, and often. However, I have learned to trust that joy is bigger than my current circumstances. That trust comes from surrendering to God's plan for my life. It's a choice. It's an action. True surrender is an active trust in the sovereignty and goodness of God.

Do you ever stop and think about how Jesus is "Lord and Savior"? I'll speak for myself here, but when I accepted God into my life, I was overcome with the knowledge that God sent his Son, Jesus, to die on the cross for me. He willingly gave each of us the gift of eternal life right there at Calvary. Knowing I did nothing to earn that gift was humbling. Once I accepted the gift of God's love and mercy, I readily and gratefully accepted his title of "Savior."

Accepting God as my Savior was easier than accepting him as Lord. At first, I didn't stop to think about the title "Lord." It was a churchy word I had heard my whole life. I knew it held power and even represented mercy, but it took me years to ponder the true meaning of the title "Lord." Honestly, I don't think I fully understood it until my son was diagnosed. I no longer had any control (not that I truly ever had it, mind you). It was the first time I truly surrendered to God. It was the first time I relinquished control to him. I remember crying and praying for God to take my pain. I didn't think I'd be able to survive watching my son deteriorate and suffer. I knew this could be our lives for years, and I wasn't strong enough to do it. It was then that I realized what "Lord" truly meant. God is Lord over my life, and what a comfort that is. He has the power and authority in my life and that of my son. We aren't powerless because we have God.

Surrendering to God is not about abandoning your freedom. Surrendering to God is giving your cares to him so you can have freedom in Christ. You can relinquish your needs, doubts, fears, hopes, and dreams to him. God doesn't need our surrender to make him more powerful. He desires our surrender so that we may inherit his power in Christ.

Reflections

But blessed is the one who trusts in the LORD,
  whose confidence is in him.
They will be like a tree planted by the water
  that sends out its roots by the stream.
It does not fear when heat comes;
  its leaves are always green.
It has no worries in a year of drought
  and never fails to bear fruit. (Jer. 17:7–8)

1. Remembering that we have to let go of something in order to receive what God wants to give us, fill out this statement: Relinquishment means letting go of the _____ so I have room to accept the _____ God has for me.

2. What is one thing you're worrying about right now? Pray and ask God to help you release it to him.

3. What attributes of God are you confident of? Which parts of his character are most trustworthy for you?

4. Which parts of God's character seem less trustworthy? Ask God to help you trust all his characteristics and plans for your life.

11

Unexpected to Designed

It might be difficult to imagine that you are perfectly designed to be the mother to your child. One of the common sayings in our world is "God gives special kids only to special people." Some of us balk at this saying, and there are quite a few opinions on it. If you don't believe us, just do an internet search. While we don't believe that any one of us is more "special" than anyone else, we do believe that our children (all of them) are a part of God's perfect plan. Most of us didn't realize what we signed up for, but we rose to the occasion of caring for our children. And now we have a choice. Just like a horse may fight the bit in its mouth or choose to submit, we have the same decision before us. We can continue to fight against what we didn't dream for our lives or choose to submit to God's design. Fighting is more painful than trusting.

Do you believe that God has perfectly fashioned your struggles to shape and mold you and to display the Creator's glorious works through you? After many years of parenting our children and having the blessing of hindsight, we've come to realize that God does perfectly orchestrate our lives. We may not understand his ways, but we can trust him. Trust comes down to noticing God's plan for our lives and choosing to have faith in him.

~~~~~~~~~

I (Amy) met and fell in love with my husband in high school. The beginning of our relationship was not very romantic. We were lab partners in a science class, and our assignment was to dissect a fetal pig together. We became good friends, fell in love, and got married. In those early days, we had so many dreams and plans for our lives. As a young married couple, we had an idea of what a good life would look like. Some of what we hoped for happened, but most of it did not. With a new husband and the starry-eyed idealism of a young bride, I had no idea what was in store for us. We couldn't have imagined that we would endure infertility, death, and heartache. We didn't know that we would be special needs parents. That young girl with her eighties hair and big dreams didn't know what was ahead, and I am glad she didn't.

After years of infertility, we were grateful to be the parents of three kids. We wanted to add to our family and felt the call to adopt. I remember receiving the thick stack of adoption forms to fill out and feeling overwhelmed. We diligently completed our home study, asked friends to write reference letters, and checked all the boxes needed to complete the application, all the while dreaming of the child who would eventually join our family.

As we waded through the papers, one form gave me pause. It was a complete list of disabilities and conditions we would be willing to accept in a child. It felt heartless to say no to any of them, but I couldn't help worrying about what we could handle. Do I want to say yes to a wheelchair or HIV? Can I handle a child with a permanent disability? How do you know before you even love or meet a child what a disability will mean in your daily life? In the end, we decided to say no to several conditions. We rationalized that we were not equipped to be special needs parents. In reality, I did not want to be a special needs mom. I don't remember what boxes we checked, but I remember saying an absolute no to fetal alcohol spectrum disorder (FASD). I had briefly read about FASD in nursing school and decided to take a hard pass on that one.

The truth is none of us know what we can handle or how any illness or disability will play out in our lives or the life of our child. There was no reported history of alcohol and drug abuse when we adopted our daughter, but over several years filled with alarming and bewildering behaviors, we learned that she had FASD and reactive attachment disorder (RAD). We became special needs parents.

This was not what we expected, planned, or signed up for (literally!). Being a mom to a child with these struggles was not what I would have put on my list of things I wanted in life. I want my child to have friends, be healthy, and thrive. I don't wish her to battle mental health issues and schedules filled with therapies and appointments. I don't want the loneliness, fatigue, and grief that come with being a special needs mom. This was not in my plan, but it was in God's.

I used to believe that if I trusted God, he would give me the desires of my heart. I thought all those desires were about getting what I wanted in life. My list included what I thought would make me happy. As I have gotten older, I have realized that the desires have changed to much deeper desires.

Today I know that my heart's desire means one thing: God. He is my hope, my life, and my light. All that is good and true is found in him. He is the deepest desire of my heart; this world and all its distractions are not. What we expected was not what we got, but there is still beauty in what God has given us. His plan is perfect for us. God invites us to come out from the burden of our unmet expectations and dwell in hope.

We often do not dwell in hope; instead, we make our home in the shelter constructed by unmet expectations and the disappointment that life is not how we wish it would be. We may not have chosen this life, but we still have choices, and one choice we can make as special needs moms is this: we can choose what deepens God's life in us. What deepens God's life in us is hope. We are invited to come home to hope.

We may not have chosen this life, but we still have choices, and one choice we can make as special needs moms is this: we can choose what deepens God's life in us.

Hope allows us to look at our lives and be transformed by the unexpected. When we live in hope, we can look at our lives as God's perfect plan for us. Our faith illuminates the darkness and gives us the capacity to live this life as special needs moms with purpose and joy, especially when our lives don't look like we thought they would. Instead of focusing on our circumstances, we need to fix our eyes on the One who walks with us. This change in perspective allows joy to bubble up from the deep well of our souls.

We do not know what life will bring. We have to trust that God will give us the grace to handle it. The truth is that most of life does not turn out as we expected. But God has designed it, and as we walk with him, he equips us for the life we have.

God has purpose and provision for the life he has given us. When we leave our lives in his loving hands, we can dwell where he has put us and be nurtured by his rich love as special needs moms.

We're familiar with the unexpected and life's plans going awry as special needs mothers. We're used to dealing with the curveballs and the fastballs, and we wish for more slow pitches. It's easy to dismiss events in our lives as chance, luck, or just the way things turned out. But have you ever taken the time to look back over your life to recognize how various decisions were arranged to place you exactly where you needed to be? Scripture relates how our days were written before our existence, and God knows each one (Ps. 139:16). He knows our personalities, our hearts' intricacies, and what we need and don't need. Life's unanticipated twists and turns are part of God's designed plan.

How do we begin to see God's design in our circumstances? First, we must acknowledge that the events we attribute to mere coincidence are God's divine interruptions in our lives. Sometimes these interruptions are subtle, other times more obvious. I (Carrie) believe God used a second-grade friend with Down syndrome, the young girl I met with spina bifida in college, and the child with autism in my first year of teaching to prepare me to be a special needs mom. When we look at the unexpected and stop dismissing it as coincidence, we will see that things didn't happen by chance but were a part of God's design.

Look for the ways God has intervened in your life. Often, we see God's miracles as only extreme answers to prayer: a diagnosed unborn baby born perfectly healthy or the healing of stage 4 four cancer. What if God's blessings are evident not only in complete restoration but also through his provision, care, and the small ways he heals? (The story I am about to share with you is rather unusual. I do not want it to make you discontent with your situation or feel more alone. It is merely a testimony of God's small miracles in my own life.)

While in college, I worked at the campus bookstore with an adult staff member who had a daughter named Erika. Erika and I met only once during those four years, but after graduation, she and I lived in the same city, attended the same church, and became fast friends after marriage to our respective fiancés. She and I began to dream of having babies and got pregnant a month apart. When I was almost two weeks overdue, and she was one week early, our sons were born sixteen hours apart in the same hospital.

When her son was three months old, he was admitted to the hospital with respiratory complications. Several months later, he came home, a medically fragile baby with a tracheostomy, ventilator, and feeding tube. Three years later, with a few other children born in between, I became pregnant with my special needs son. After his prenatal diagnosis of Chiari type 2 malformation, I read a book about it. I learned about the rare symptoms caused by this malformation in the brain: obstructive and central sleep apnea, stridor (making noise while breathing), feeding and swallowing disorders, and reflux. The book discussed how some infants experience vocal cord paralysis and need a tracheostomy.[1] I was pretty familiar with a trach, ventilator, and feeding tube because of Erika and her son. I knew firsthand what life looked like with a medically fragile baby and home nursing care. It was tough. Erika's life was one I didn't want, and I diligently prayed it wouldn't happen to me. Yet three months after birth, Toby came home as a medically fragile baby with the same issues.

God didn't answer my prayers in the way I expected. There wasn't miraculous healing, yet there was miraculous provision through a friend who had walked a similar journey. God intervened not by healing my son but by providing friendship well before I knew it would be needed.

Maybe you're reading this and thinking, *That's all well and good, Carrie, but I don't have any stories like that.* May I encourage you to ask God to reveal what you've possibly dismissed as coincidence and see it for what it truly is? See the small victories for what they are, God's mercies raining down. Whether it's a change with your child, strengthened faith, a deeper relationship, or any other beautiful gift, God masterminds perfect plans.

I won't pretend it wasn't devastating to discover that our son had the malformation after I had fervently prayed for it not to happen. I struggled in my prayer life after that because, if God already had his mind made up, what sense did it make to pray for things? I learned to lament God telling me no, and I begged him to reveal how he did provide. It wasn't a coincidence that I read that book before our son was born. And it wasn't a coincidence that I had met Erika. God prepared me for what was to come.

God shows up in the small. He desires to give good gifts to his children and for us to recognize and accept those gifts, even when they aren't what we expect.

While I was pregnant with Toby, testing revealed that despite my prayers for a completely healthy baby, my child would have spina bifida. God had chosen me to be a special needs mom. As a result, years later, I rarely prayed for any healing for our son. During a time between hospital stays, a friend shared that she had been praying for me. I almost told her not to because we didn't need prayers right then, but the Holy Spirit revealed that we always need other people praying and that I shouldn't dismiss her. I needed to recognize the ways God had healed and ask him for what I desired. In my mind, healing meant our son could walk. That hadn't happened. I hadn't seen the small ways God worked because I was looking for significant miracles. I wasn't asking for the small things because I thought he worked only in the big and remarkable things. He doesn't. He works in the small things too.

Sometimes we spend so much time moving forward that we don't take the time to reflect on where we've been. God has given you healing and beauty in your own life. It might be the doctor who truly understands, the empathy of a friend, or the peace in your heart. The beauty in your situation may be less about your child's healing and more about the change in your heart. Look for the ways God has revealed his design in the small. You will be overwhelmed by his generous gifts.

I (Sara) am a planner by nature. My calendar is color coded by family member. My business even has its own color for each of my clients. My calendar is mapped out in fifteen-minute increments, and I have been known to schedule showers. (Unfortunately, I'm not joking.) I appreciate a good spreadsheet, and anything that organizes is something I want to try.

When we were handed our son's diagnosis, my world flipped on its head. There was no organizing the type of chaos that ensued. I could no longer make sense of my life. I pleaded for God to make sense of it. I wanted to know his plan because I couldn't see past the pain.

I won't bore you with all our woes. But let's just say that life has been less than splendid at times. It can be especially overwhelming when we focus on the permanency of the diagnoses and everything we will have to deal with throughout this journey. When I realized that Duchenne was forever a part of our lives (until it won't be, which is too final to contemplate), I ran straight into that brick wall of reality. Hard. And it hurt.

I realized that even though we all deal with Duchenne, it's TJ who will have to live with it. It was terrifying to know I would have to watch my child struggle with this disease and that there was nothing I could do to protect him from it.

I asked God how I would possibly be strong enough for everything that we would face, every daily challenge or setback, with no break in sight. Even though I knew it is his strength, not mine, that would get me through it, I just didn't see how I would survive it all. My human brain couldn't comprehend it. I was viewing my life in the here and now. I was looking at everything that was happening negatively to my family. Still, I was also trying to look ahead to try to avoid any surprises.

On days when my mind gets the best of me, I rely solely on faith. When I get too caught up with trying to map out my next steps, I am reminded that God has already mapped out the entire path. Not only has he mapped my course but he has also already equipped me to navigate it.

God gently directs our paths if we are still enough to stop and listen for his guidance. One such redirect happened at our kitchen table one ordinary evening. Everyone was occupied with our typical evening routines. TJ was sitting at the kitchen table. He loves to draw. He would often sit down with his tongue hanging out the side of his mouth and create for long stretches of time. I walked by the kitchen table and looked over his shoulder. I asked, "What is it?" And he replied, "I'm not done yet!" He then covered up his drawing with his arm, bent his head down, and continued. He said, "I'll show it to you when I'm done, Mom! It'll be so much better then." I adequately apologized and left him to finish his masterpiece. As I walked away smiling to myself, I was struck by a realization. I paused and turned back to look at my son. I recognized that I had been asking the same question of God.

How often do we stop mid-drawing and ask God, "What is this?! Why? It doesn't make sense! God, I just don't see it!" In my kitchen, through a simple, everyday conversation I had with my son, God simply answered, "Be patient. I'm not done yet. It's going to be so much better when I'm finished."

My grandma used to quilt (she loved making cute baby quilts with blocks of colorful animals she would hand stitch). As a little girl, I would play under the quilt frame she put up on sawhorses. I remember thinking how crazy all the quilt blocks looked from below. They looked like a jumbled mess. I could vaguely distinguish a big purple animal—it kind of looked like a bear. But my sister and I would always look at her work after she was done for the day, and I was always amazed at how beautiful and neat the front was compared to the back. After my son told me about his picture, this memory also reminded me that God is stitching our lives together. What we see may just be the crazy, messy back side. But when he's finished, the finished product will be amazing and full of the love he put into it.

So often, we want to see the big picture; we want to see the finished product before it's time. We don't see the potential because we are too busy looking at the messy parts. We also find that we are tempted to take over when life gets difficult. In those moments, it is vital to remember that God is the Master Creator. Trust him. He will always be able to do more than we could ever imagine.

Life is uncertain. Life is messy, and it doesn't always make sense. What may not make sense to us, what may appear to be an unexpected mistake, is something God will use to design some of his most remarkable work. Our lives are a thing of beauty, and God is the Master Artist. He is patiently and diligently painting each and every stroke with love. He is stitching and weaving his mercy, love, and grace into the design of our stories. He is making everything perfect in his time. He's not done yet! We need to trust and be patient while he transforms us. It's going to be amazing!

Reflections

Being confident of this, that he who began a good work in you will carry it on to completion until the day of Christ Jesus. (Phil. 1:6)

1. Reflect on your life and think about the events you considered coincidences. Can you see how some were actually a part of God's plan?

2. Look up the word *hope* in the Psalms. Write down two verses that encourage you the most. How does hope help you see God's perfect design in your circumstances?

3. Write down all the things that are burdening you today. Next to each burden, write what is actually your responsibility related to that burden (some may say none). Pray Matthew 11:28–29, filling in the blanks below:

"Come to me, [your name], who are weary and burdened with [name burden], and I [Jesus] will give [your name] rest. Take my yoke upon [your name] and learn from me, for I am gentle and humble in heart, and [your name] will find rest for [your name] soul. I release this [name burden] to you."

4. Write down a few items that were the desires of your heart before your child came along. What are the desires of your heart now? How are they similar to or different from what you're living now?

12

Disappointment
to Gratitude

It can be hard to think of anything to be grateful for amid disappointment. Whether it is a challenging day, week, month, or season, special needs moms live a life they did not anticipate. These situations can evoke feelings of discouragement and disappointment. Scripture passages that encourage gratitude in all things can be disheartening and seem impossible to follow. Often, we compare our lives to those of others, and that leaves us feeling resentful. When we focus on the negative, we miss the beauty of this life. We need a change of perspective. We can shift our gaze from the circumstances before us to look for God's grace.

We can experience gratitude, not a "grin and bear it" forced gratitude but a genuine gratitude, in our unique lives. We can look at our lives as special needs moms and see God's goodness even amid challenges. We can focus on the gifts of his love and presence in our lives. Life may not look like we thought it would, but we are deeply loved and held by him no matter what.

───※───

Reminders to practice gratitude are everywhere. Drive to a craft store, and you will see hand-painted signs encouraging us to "Be grateful" or "Have a thankful heart." As children, we were told to be grateful for our food, toys, and homes. The Bible is filled with verses on giving thanks. On the surface, I (Amy) think we can easily list what we are grateful for. We are thankful for our homes, food, family, country, and faith. These are all things that are easy to write down on a gratitude list. I have kept many a list in my life, and if you would have asked me, I could have named several things. But riding shotgun to my gratitude list was a healthy dose of ingratitude. That ingratitude was rooted in disappointment.

Several years ago, I went to considerable trouble to plan a birthday party for a relative. I prepared the food, arranged the guests, and ordered a gift. On the day of the party, after everyone was gone, my relative said to me, "Thanks, but this isn't really what I wanted." Ouch.

I was hurt by that, of course. But I have thought about that conversation many times. Sometimes I write in my gratitude journal, "Thank you, God, for my family, home, and the beautiful sunset," but in my heart, I am saying, "but this isn't what I wanted." My disappointment overrides any genuine gratitude.

It isn't that I am not grateful for my house, husband, and kids. These are all things for which I am deeply thankful. It's just that there is also so much hard happening. My life as a special needs mom can be so overwhelming that it is difficult to stop and write down what I am grateful for. Some days it is impossible even to stop and notice. Other days I can pray prayers of gratitude and still be filled with ingratitude. Being thankful is challenging.

Can you relate? How do we overcome the disappointment when we see other moms whose lives are not dictated by doctor appointments and treatments? How can we be grateful when our child is not included because of their behavior or disability? How do we root out ingratitude when it seems that everyone else is living a life of relative ease and we are so overwhelmed that we don't know how to make it one more day?

Honestly, it's hard to stop and breathe in gratitude in the middle of life as a special needs mom. It's so much easier to be disappointed in a life filled with stress, behavioral issues, and treatment. We have to remember that gratitude is not just about a list of blessings and the things that are going well in our lives. What leads to true contentment is living life with gratitude and fullness in the midst of the broken. Gratitude—deep gratitude, the kind that changes your heart—causes you to open your heart to see the gift of love in life. Everything we need to overcome our disappointment is rooted in gratitude. We can be thankful even in the midst of difficult times.

> **What leads to true contentment is living life with gratitude and fullness in the midst of the broken.**

Writing down what we are thankful for is an excellent practice. But to get a true heart of gratitude, authentic gratitude that cannot be influenced or dimmed by our circumstances, we have to recognize our disappointment. Authentic thankfulness requires us to go deeper than hand-painted reminders to be grateful and gratitude jour-nals. Before we can be genuinely grateful, we have to recognize our ingratitude.

Ingratitude is when we look at our lives and are not satis-fied with what we see. Recognizing this is the first step. Then we can ask God to forgive us and give us the grace to notice all the blessings he bestows on us.

When I am ungrateful, I don't recognize Christ around me or the way God's love is evident in my life. One helpful reminder is that even in the midst of what is challenging, we are being held in love. People love us imperfectly. Life doesn't always look like we want it to, and we have so many reasons to be disappointed. But in all of this, we are held in love. There has never been a time in your life as a special needs mom when God's loving arms did not embrace you.

Not once.

Not the day you received the diagnosis and everything changed.

Not when the invitations do not come and you feel lonely.

Not the nights you sit by a hospital bed, or the evenings you are frustrated as you fill out another long insurance form.

This life may not be what you wanted or expected, but in every single one of these moments, you are held in love. You can trust that place of love. You can look at all that disappoints you and release it to God.

Remembering we are held in love shifts our focus from gifts to the Giver. We can move past the pain and sink deeply into the life we have. Remembering that God's love holds us is how we stay rooted in gratitude. When we look at our lives through the lens of gratitude, we realize we have enough. We can understand that God's gifts are not random. They are intentional.

Gratitude opens us up to grace. Gratitude is essential to moving forward and walking this path as a special needs mom.

As a mom of a child who doesn't keep up with their peers mentally, physically, and emotionally, you can easily grow discontent with your circumstances. Your grief escalates every time you're asked to fill out a questionnaire for an IEP meeting or at the pediatrician's office. Sadness and disappointment overwhelm you as the growing list of "no" or "does not apply" boxes are checked. I (Carrie) am always tempted to draw a dot-to-dot picture with the boxes or mark things out with a giant red X! Alas, I'm a rule follower and never do that, but I'm so tempted.

This life is full of disappointment and grief as we compare our child to others. It's even more complicated when friends or family dismiss our pain because grief is an ongoing part of this journey. No matter our child's age or diagnosis, we mourn disappointments sometimes daily. Let's admit that disappointment isn't always the most powerful word. Sometimes it's sorrow, grief, or anger we're feeling.

To not allow seeds of disappointment to sprout into weeds of bitterness, we need to take the first step toward gratitude. This doesn't mean we ignore our pain and see the glass as half full. Gratitude requires lamenting our losses with God. God wants us to cry out to him. "I waited patiently for the Lord; he turned to me and heard my cry. He lifted me out of the slimy pit, out of the mud and mire; he set my feet on a rock and gave me a firm place to stand" (Ps. 40:1–2). God is near, and he hears your cries. Even though it doesn't always feel like it, his face is turned toward you. You can sink into the pit of discouragement or choose to invite him into your pain, pouring out even your anger to him. He knows what's in there anyway, so don't be afraid to call out to him.

When our son was first diagnosed, I will never forget sitting in the car and my husband saying, "If not us, then who?" I honestly wasn't sure what he meant at first. Part of me, now, wants to punch him. His point was that we have the faithful companion of Jesus to walk on this journey with us. We aren't alone. God is with us. Our happiness can fluctuate based on our circumstances, but joy comes from the Lord and keeping our gaze on him. We may not be rescued from the fire, but he's in it with us.

Disappointment and gratitude are not mutually exclusive. You can experience both emotions at the same time. It's not an either/or situation but rather a both/and. First Thessalonians tells us, "Give thanks in all circumstances; for this is God's will for you in Christ Jesus" (5:18). This may seem like a pretty hard ask. But notice that this verse tells us to give thanks not *for* our circumstances but *in* them.

Life looked pretty bleak when our son was in intensive care as an infant. We weren't sure if he would survive. I remember experiencing fear and sadness and being overwhelmed by our situation, but I was also encouraged by the Holy Spirit to record all I had to be thankful for during that time. The list started small, and I begrudgingly wrote down obvious items. I was alive. My son was alive. Then I began to dig deeper. I listed things such as not paying for parking, a waived hospital copay, a meal, and childcare for our other two young boys. Then the list began to gain momentum. By the time I was finished, I was blown away by how many gifts God had given me, even amid the pain.

He is Jehovah Jireh, our Provider. He is providing in ways we sometimes don't notice. I encourage you today to start the practice of gratitude. Again, just because we're grateful doesn't mean we won't also be disappointed when we face hardships. It's important to let our frustrations and grief breathe but not be in charge.[1] We shouldn't stuff our feelings down, but neither should we allow them to drive the train of our lives. When we take the time every day to practice gratitude and search for God's gifts, our perspective changes from what we lack to the abundance God has bountifully poured out in our lives.

I believe it's also essential to allow others' stories of courage to encourage us and persuade us to see the goodness of God. The more we know about God's work, the more we can appreciate his kindness and generosity. When I was a girl, I was fascinated by the story of five missionaries (Jim Elliot, Nate Saint, Roger Youdarian, Peter Fleming, and Ed McCully) who left their comfortable lives to live in the jungle of Ecuador to share about God with the Waodoni people, who had never heard about him. This was no easy task, as the reputation of the people they wanted to reach was one of brutality. They often were referred to as Aucas, meaning savages or killers.

Unfortunately, in 1956, after several instances of friendly contact with the jungle people, unexpectedly, the five missionary men were slaughtered by the Waodani on Palm Beach. God used the deaths of all five men to change this tribe for eternity. Afterward, two of the men's family members went back and lived among the people, translated the Bible into their language, and shared Christ with them. Mincaye, who was involved in killing Steve Saint's father, Nate, became a

God follower. Eventually, he became like a father to Steve and a grandfather to his children. Steve and his sister were baptized in the jungle river by another one of the miraculously changed men.

In his book *End of the Spear*, Steve relates the many details of the killing and how too many pieces fit together perfectly for it not to have been a part of God's perfect plan. He said, "I have seen firsthand that much good has come from it. Only God could have fashioned such an incredible story from such a tragic event. I could not begin to record the thousands of people who have told me that God used what happened on Palm Beach to change the course of lives for good."[2]

God has used this story in my own life to shape how I view suffering and pain and to teach me how to choose joy amid grief and gratitude in the midst of disappointment. Just recently, I learned that the date the men were killed was one day after my birth date. It was one more assurance that God's plans go beyond the immediate families involved and are a testimony for others to "see and fear [that word means awe-struck respect] the LORD and put their trust in him" (Ps. 40:3).

It all started with a challenge. To know me (Sara) is to know I love a good challenge, and I rarely back down from one. During what was probably the lowest point in my life, I honestly could not muster a grateful heart. I felt like my life was crumbling around me. There I was, standing in the middle of unrecognizable wreckage that I was realizing was my life. How did this happen? My first reaction was to frantically try to fortify the walls I had started to build to protect my fragile heart. Every time I would try to repair one wall, grabbing bricks and shoving them in place, another wall behind me would begin to crumble little by little. Some walls were blown to smithereens, left in shambles, and completely unable to be repaired. I had no idea what to do, had nowhere to turn, and was utterly exhausted trying to fix the splinters of my life on my own.

When someone says, "My heart hurt," I now understand what they mean. I found myself lying on the floor of my closet, alone, crying, until I felt ill. I had never felt so heartbroken and alone. I was truly lost. However, I can look back and see that it was at that moment, in my closet, that I began to heal.

All I knew was that I couldn't keep living the way I was living. Literally. Honestly, I was scared. When I cried out to God that I couldn't take any more, I believe it was at that moment that God comforted me by reassuring me that it was never mine to carry alone anyway. I was building barriers that weren't meant to be built, and the walls that belonged were his to construct.

I didn't want to continue how I was living—always waiting for the other shoe to drop. I was in self-preservation mode. I wasn't going to let anything else disappoint me. Here's the thing with building walls so nothing terrible can reach you again: those same walls also keep out the blessings. I had closed off my heart because I knew one more disappointment would shatter it. Closing off our hearts to the pain only hardens them to our purpose. I was so busy protecting my heart and building my walls so high that I couldn't see the blessings

Here's the thing with building walls so nothing terrible can reach you again: those same walls also keep out the blessings.

around me. I was missing the good in life because I was too busy working on removing the bad.

That moment in the closet was pivotal for me. In the depths of my soul, I knew that I was at a turning point. I could either be a woman, mom, and wife who was negative and bitter and would drag everyone down with me, or I could be the woman I was called to be, the woman I wanted to be. I knew what I wanted, but I didn't know how to get it.

The first step was to pull myself up off the floor. I remember getting to my knees, ready to push myself up to standing, but staying there instead with both knees on the floor. I began to pray as I had never prayed before. I'm sure what I gave God was a torrent of nonsense. I am grateful that my nonsense was exactly what God wanted to hear. He was the only One able to make sense of everything I was feeling.

I remember telling God that I wanted to be a better woman. I told him I didn't want to build walls again unless he was the Master Builder. I didn't want to walk through life miserable because I knew I would set the tone for myself and my family. I wanted to be a better daughter to him and believe in his goodness again. I wanted to live like I trusted him with an open heart. I was honest with God. I told him I didn't feel all those things—yet. I was still upset with the hand I had been dealt in life, but at least I knew I wanted to play again. I didn't see how this was all going to happen; I just knew God would need to be in control if it was going to happen. I needed to get out of his way.

So I pulled myself off the floor, both literally and figuratively. In typical Sara fashion, I started researching how to be happy and content. Yes, I actually researched that. I read an online challenge to write down at least three things I was grateful for, and to do that for thirty days. I figured perhaps focusing on a few good things each day would pull me out of whatever depression had settled into my soul. It was worth trying. It couldn't hurt, right?

The first few days I wrote down things like coffee, sunshine, comfortable flip-flops, not being late, or holding my tongue when someone ticked me off. About a week in, I thought the things I was listing were silly.

There were days when I would get to the end of the day, sigh, and think that I needed to write down a few things just to fulfill the challenge for the day. I was checking the to-do box of gratitude. Knowing I was missing the point of the challenge, I decided to search for things to be grateful for throughout each day. I was going to seek them out and keep track intentionally. I was going to make it through the thirty days, and I would win at it!

Then the strangest thing happened. I was so busy searching for something to be thankful for that I forgot to build my crumbling walls again. I had taken my focus and, therefore, my energy away from life's disappointments and redirected them to God's abundant grace.

I would be lying to say that this thirty-day challenge magically healed me. Once the month was over, I was still hurting. Life still had disappointments and heartache. I found myself trying to build walls from time to time. I wasn't always positive, and everything wasn't sunshine and unicorns. However, those thirty days taught me that gratitude is a matter of intentionality.

Don't misunderstand me; I don't believe we can force ourselves to have a grateful heart. I don't think God wants that either. However, we can intentionally turn to God, thanking him for his gifts. And when we are struggling to see the good, we can ask for his help to recognize it.

Gratitude is not the absence of disappointment. Gratitude is the ability to acknowledge life's disappointments while trusting God's goodness. God is in control; he is sovereign, merciful, and good, and his gifts are plentiful because he so lavishly loves us.

Reflections

Give thanks to the LORD, for he is good;
his love endures forever. (Ps. 118:1)

1. What disappointments do you need to lament? How can lamenting help you accept your life as a special needs mom?
2. What are three things you are thankful for today?
3. List areas in your life where you are still holding on to ingratitude. Take these areas to God and ask him to show you how to root them out. Remember that he holds you in his loving hands.
4. Remembering we are held in love is central to gratitude. Meditate on Scripture passages about God's love and presence. (Pss. 23; 136; 139 are some examples and great places to start.)

Bonus Chapter

Navigating a Crisis

We are very familiar with navigating crises, from medical emergencies to behavioral issues, and dealing with schools, insurance, and catastrophes. Special needs moms make up the best crisis intervention team. But sometimes these events rock our foundation and make us question our abilities, God's faithfulness, and our faith. There's no right or wrong way to navigate emergencies, but being prepared spiritually, emotionally, and mentally can help. You also need a team of helpers around as your support network. Do not face situations alone. Whether it's a spouse, trusted family member, friend, or therapist, be willing to share your burdens with them. Have a go-to text group ready to pray on your behalf. If you don't have that type of support, please pray for God to provide the support you need. He cares and doesn't wish for you to be alone.

Next, make a list of rhythms, events, or tasks that help you rest in the midst of a crisis. When life is calm, pay attention to your body to learn what drains your energy and what refuels you. These rhythms of life are what you should place on this list.

Lastly, remember what is true about God and utilize periods of peace to dig your roots deep into God's Word. Create a list of God's names and their meanings and how they specifically apply to you, your child, and your situation. For example, El Roi means the God who sees. Write how you feel seen by God. What is true about God is true when life is going well and when it's disrupted. He is our constant source of truth, strength, grace, mercy, joy, and peace. Draw life from him.

Last year I (Amy) was standing in the emergency room while my child was admitted with another mental health issue. My eyes were tired and scratchy, and I felt exhausted from the hospital's constant noise and harsh lighting. I was waiting for my husband to show up, and I did not even have the energy to text anyone to pray. As I stood there in yet another crisis, I felt sad, overwhelmed, and lonely. This was not my first time experiencing a crisis. Over the years, I have stood in doctors' offices, principals' offices, therapists' offices, and hospital rooms. I have heard news I didn't know how to process or even understand. Amid this new crisis, I had to remember what I knew to be true about God to make it through another difficult situation. When all seems dark, I want to remember that no matter how dark it gets, Jesus is the Light of the world, and he dispels the darkness.

We know what it is like to have a child wake us up in the middle of the night. We can stumble half asleep and lead them back to bed in the dark without running into the furniture. We can do this because we're familiar with all the furniture in our homes. We know what each room looks like in the daylight, so we can navigate that space in the dark.

I have learned to navigate the darkness of a crisis by remembering what I know to be true about God in the light. In the midst of the disorientation at the beginning of an emergency, look for the signposts. Signs orient us to what we know to be true. We know what God looks like when the light is on. We can let his familiar beauty and grace pull us through a crisis.

God draws near to us in times of trouble when we are disoriented and afraid and don't know how to handle the dark. In a crisis, plans are interrupted and our familiar days are not what we envisioned. Whether you are facing a crisis that has you rushing to the hospital unexpectedly or one that has been a long time coming, you probably have only a glimpse of the brewing storm. Remember that God is with you—no matter what. Regardless of what you are feeling, be it fear, grief, or loneliness, you have enough light to navigate the darkness. Look for what is familiar, and stand firm on the solid ground that Jesus is your Light and Life.

During a crisis, these are the truths you can remember about God. These truths will be the lights that guide you in the darkness.

God provides. In a crisis, remember how God provides in these moments. His provision can be seen in health care professionals who help your family, in the friend ready to drop a meal at your door, and in the prayers sent to heaven on your behalf. Once you start remembering all the needs that have been met, you will be surprised, and you won't be able to see life any other way.

God is present. We can be hopeful even in the midst of a crisis because God is always with us. He promises that he is with us in the storm. He shelters us under his wings. Crises will come, but in our troubles, God is present. The next time you are in the hospital or another place of crisis, walk to a window and look up at the sky. Allow yourself a moment to pray and be still and acknowledge that God is with you.

God offers rest. Rest can be difficult in a crisis. But it is not impossible. We often think, *When I get through this, I will rest.* Even in a crisis, when the water threatens to overtake us, we can trust Jesus for moments of rest. We need to pay attention to our bodies and rest when we can. This may require taking a break, praying, and being silent for a few minutes. We may have to accept help. We special needs moms have a hard time receiving support for some reason. We think we have to do it all. During a crisis, others often offer assistance. Say yes to those offers. They are ways that God provides you with rest.

God gives peace. He promises to give us peace. It is a fact, the truth, a done deal. We may not always feel it, but that doesn't mean it isn't there. Having peace doesn't mean there isn't a crisis, all the problems are solved, and the kids are tucked in bed. We can learn to experience peace regardless of what is swirling around us. Remind yourself that Christ offers his peace and that his love and presence are always with you, no matter what. His peace is a light in the dark.

As a special needs mom, you will probably experience more than one crisis in the future. You may feel overwhelmed and scared. But know that you can rely on God's provision, presence, rest, and peace.

In the process of writing this book, as you can imagine, all three of us experienced a crisis with our kids. I (Carrie) have personally lost count of the number of crises I've experienced. So what can you do when a crisis hits?

First of all, thank the Lord for your fight response and the adrenaline release that protects you. Then try to rein in your emotions in order to think clearly. You need the ability to process information and sometimes make life-altering decisions, so you can't fall apart. In our situation, my son is mentally age appropriate, and he readily reads my face and emotions, so my guard is up with him too. I'm not saying that I never cry in front of him, because I have. We have cried together too, but I do my best not to verbally vomit every worry I have in front of him because then he has to process that too. I need to explain things to him in ways he can understand so he begins to take ownership of medical decisions.

Next, as you work to navigate a crisis, it's important not to panic and to stay in your body. Remember the truth about what is happening right now. Feel your feet on the floor, look at your surroundings, and take deep breaths. This is called grounding. In traumatic situations, we forget to breathe and can become disoriented.[1] It's essential to focus on only right now and the current place you're in.

Once you're grounded, focus on only the next small step. Maybe you need to pack a bag to rush to the hospital or find a pen and paper to write something down. Just do the very next thing. Don't allow your mind to imagine every worst-case scenario. God's Word is a lamp to your feet and a light to your path. Typically, flashlights don't shine too far down the road, but they give you enough clarity to take the next step on the trail. In the middle of a crisis, keep your mind on the next thing you need to do and put one foot in front of the other.

Next, pray. One of the spiritual practices I've learned from my cohost Sara is the breath prayer. Breathe out your fears: "I'm alone and afraid." Then breathe in the truth about God's character: "He is with me." I admit that I cannot spend a lot of time in deep prayer with God when my son is hospitalized. I know this may seem strange, but I have found that I mentally fall apart if I focus too much on grieving and lamenting in those moments. It's almost like I have to hold back my emotions and rely on others to storm the gates of heaven on our behalf. When I allow myself to become completely open and intimate with God, I break down. This prevents me from thinking clearly. So instead I focus on short prayers. I try to open my morning in prayer and have an ongoing conversation with God throughout the day.

Remember two things if you ever feel like you can't pray because of the fear of opening the floodgates. First, share your burdens with others so that they can pray on your behalf. This requires vulnerability. Often, we want to handle everything on our own, but we were created for community. There's power in having others pray for us. If you're willing to share your story, and it's appropriate to your family situation, you will be amazed by the number of people willing to carry your burdens. People you don't even know may also lift you up in prayer. This is the body of Christ at work. If your child doesn't want the details shared, you're less inclined to be open, or you're facing a delicate situation, find a few close people whom you trust to be your prayer warriors. If you don't have such people, pray for God to give them to you. Second, remember that the Spirit is interceding for you even when you don't know what to ask for. Romans 8:26 promises, "In the same way, the Spirit helps us in our weakness. We do not know what we ought to pray for, but the Spirit himself intercedes for us through wordless groans." The Holy Spirit will intercede for you, especially when you don't know what or how to pray.

As the crisis continues, so does the difficulty of keeping family and friends informed of what is going on. I recommend using a website like CaringBridge or keeping a blog. I kept a site for my son for many years, and I found it helpful. It freed me from the burden of having to text or call multiple people, so it was less stressful. Repeating the traumatic situation you've just experienced can be emotionally and physically exhausting, so find a way to inform your family and friends in bulk. When keeping the site, I also found I had to process the day's events to explain them coherently. This caused me to ask a nurse or a doctor more questions, usually resulting in a greater understanding and better advocating for our child. Sometimes close family or friends would ask clarification questions, and I would write them down for the next day.

Whether you feel comfortable sharing openly or keep information close, please keep a journal, whether written or auditory. This will help you process information. Essential details you write down now are bits of information you may need later.

In a crisis, it's also really crucial to allow people to help. You're not meant to go this alone. Be honest about what you need. If someone offers to help, tell them what you need. A few practical ways are meals, house cleaning, running other kids to activities, bringing you items you need in the hospital, and delivering takeout. Some hospitals have gift cards people can purchase on your behalf to pay for the cafeteria or parking. When we fail to share our burdens, we cause others to miss out on blessings. I've often heard and experienced that those who take mission trips get more out of them than the people they serve. That's also true about those helping you.

When we fail to share our burdens, we cause others to miss out on blessings.

Lastly, expect that after the crisis has passed, you will experience grief. Just expect it. Half the battle in life is knowing what to expect. It may not come for weeks or months, but it will come. A small situation will make you feel exceedingly sad, angry, or both, and then you will say to yourself, "Carrie told me grief was going to come, and here it is." Then go back and read chapter 2 about dealing with grief.

One day, in passing, I (Sara) mentioned to a friend that I didn't know what I would write for this chapter. Crisis? My coauthors had dealt with significant life issues over the past year or so. What was I possibly going to write about? Making something up seemed . . . well, not appropriate (and yes, it did briefly cross my mind).

This friend chuckled and started listing things that had up-ended our lives. She said, "Um, your husband losing his job? How about having to change TJ's medical team? Or your own health issues?" Okay, point taken. That's a lot, but a crisis? All of that was intense and stressful and had me in tears more than a few times, but I didn't feel any of it was a crisis per se.

The word *crisis* just seems so dramatic. So the word-nerd in me looked up the definition of *crisis*. A crisis is defined as "(1) a stage in a sequence of events at which the trend of all future events, especially for better or for worse, is determined;

turning point; (2) a condition of instability or danger, as in social, economic, political, or international affairs, leading to a decisive change; or (3) a dramatic emotional or circumstantial upheaval in a person's life."[2]

Okay, yep. Crisis seemed fitting.

My complete lack of self-awareness of my own family's crises got me thinking. I know what a crisis is, so why didn't I recognize it? Have I become so accustomed to upheavals, turning points, and instability that I no longer recognize them? Am I numb to crises in daily life?

Part of this is caused by what caregivers go through every day. We are in a constant state of vigilance. Traumatic events, stressful situations, and crises seem to come at us consistently. We live in a constant state of anticipated stress.

So I don't feel that I was unaware of or numb to our circumstances. I was perfectly aware that my husband was laid off after twenty-two years with the same company. Not only did we lose our primary source of income but our insurance was also impacted. Saying we were concerned about facing significant changes to our son's health care was an understatement. I'd be lying if I said I didn't worry. Here's the thing, though: I wasn't fearful.

After years of soul work, I have found ways to help me feel grounded in God's truth, even during the most tumultuous times. I have a therapist I trust; I have friends who will sit in that space of worry, sadness, frustration, and anxiety that comes with crises; I have Christian friends who speak the truth in love over my life; and I have faith that God is with me. Always.

I often remind myself in moments of upheaval or crisis that I don't have to search for God. He's already there, with me. I may not understand or like the situation we're in at that moment, but I know God is with me.

One of my favorite stories in the Bible is about Shadrach, Meshach, and Abednego in the book of Daniel. These three men were Jewish captives of the Babylonian king Nebuchadnezzar. They refused to bow down to a gold image built to reflect the king's power and prestige, so they were bound and thrown into a fiery furnace. When the king looked in the furnace, he was astonished that the three were somehow unbound and unharmed and that a fourth man was with them in the fire. The story continues that the king called the men out of the furnace and recognized God's deliverance of them because God was with them in the fire. The king then promoted them to a higher office and decreed that their God be worshiped.

One of my favorite parts of this story is what the three men say before being thrown in the fire. When asked to defend themselves for not bowing down and worshiping the king's gods and the gold statue, the three reply:

> O Nebuchadnezzar, we do not need to defend ourselves before you. If we are thrown into the blazing furnace, the God whom we serve is able to save us. He will rescue us from your power, Your Majesty. But even if he doesn't, we want to make it clear to you, Your Majesty, that we will never serve your gods or worship the gold statue you have set up. (Dan. 3:16–18 NLT)

I think it's safe to say that Shadrach, Meshach, and Abednego were in a crisis. They had to be worried or scared. It had to be a stressful situation. *But even though*, they were confident in God. Their response was that God could save them, *but even if he didn't*, their faith was unshakable.

They knew God would save them—somehow. They were confident that even if God didn't deliver them from the fiery pit, they could trust in God's power, goodness, and mercy. I often stop and think about that level of faith.

When I am in the middle of a crisis and all I want is for God to remove the fire—remove the pain, the anguish, the stress, or the obstacles—am I going to believe that God will rescue me from the fire? *Even if he doesn't,* am I going to trust God to be there in the fire with me? Am I going to believe that God will be my ultimate salvation no matter the crises life throws at me?

There are several lessons we can learn from these three young Jewish men.

1. Trials do not mean that God is absent. He is always with you and will protect you even in the hottest fire.
2. Even if God does not remove the crisis, be assured that he will walk you through it. So stand firm in your faith.
3. Your story matters. Just like God used those three Jewish men to change a king's life, so he can use you to profoundly impact someone else's. Maybe watching you in the fire will strengthen someone's faith.
4. Jesus is with you before, during, and after every trial. Perhaps instead of spending so much energy searching for a way out of the fire, take hold of Jesus, who is already there, holding you.

When we feel that life has bound us and thrown us into a fiery pit of crazy and messy circumstances, we can stand firm in our faith that God will rescue us. We can ask God to remove the crisis, *but even if he doesn't,* we can take comfort that Jesus is standing in the fire with us.

Reflections

For God alone my soul waits in silence;
  from him comes my salvation.
He alone is my rock and my salvation,
  my fortress; I shall not be greatly shaken. (Ps.
  62:1–2 ESV)

1. What is true about God right now in your life? Make a list as it applies to your situation.
2. What crises shake you the most (feeling out of control, medical, behavioral, etc.)? What is one thing you can plan to do the next time that event occurs that will help maintain your stability and give you peace?
3. Make a list of the ways you can rest your mind when a crisis occurs (praying Scripture, journaling, a breath prayer, a walk, etc.). Write out on note cards a few Scripture verses that are your greatest comfort for you to have with you.
4. Write down a list of friends you can turn to in a crisis. If you haven't already, send them a text or email to ask them to be your prayer warriors. Identify friends who will listen when a crisis comes and have them on your favorites list in your phone.

Acknowledgments

We are so grateful for the opportunity to write this book. This book would not have been possible without the support of others. We would like to thank those who offered encouragement and guidance in the process.

To our hope*writer Mastermind coaches, Gary Morland, Brian J. Dixon, and Emily P. Freeman: Thank you for teaching and encouraging us.

To our 2020 Mastermind cohort: Thank you for being women who continue to write words that matter and for cheering us on.

To our wonderful editor, Rachel McRae: Thank you for helping us craft our words, for championing our message, and for your love for the special needs community.

To Sadina Grody Brott, Olivia Peitsch, Melinda Timmer, and the team at Revell: Thank you for making this book a reality.

To Andrea Doering: Thank you for listening to our book idea and seeing promise.

To Karen Neumair and Credo Communications: Thank you for helping us navigate this process.

To Ann Kroeker: Thank you for encouragement and editing.

To Anna Brown Kwan: Thank you for being our first editor.

To our *Take Heart* audience: Thank you for listening and supporting us.

From Amy:

First of all, to David: On each step of this journey, you have been by my side. Thank you for loving me, supporting me, and making me laugh. You are my only one.

To Davis, Anna, and Evan: You three . . . what would I do without your deep thoughts, great conversations, and shenanigans? I am so grateful you are not only my children but also my dear friends. Thank you for loving me and encouraging me. I love you deeply.

To Davis: Thank you for your kindness and gentle presence that brings calm.

To Anna: Thank you for the edits, listening to my despair over technology, and fixing my run-on sentences! I owe it all to you.

To Evan: You taught the three of us how to record a podcast and endured many dumb questions! Thanks for your patience, for cheering me on, and for always making me laugh.

To Ella: You bring joy, and I am glad you are my daughter.

To CGB and IPB: Please know you are loved and seen by our good God. Dad and I love you.

To Julie, my first and most dedicated fan: I miss you.

To Heather and Scott: What would I do without you? Thank you for being the hands and feet of Christ in my life and for calling me Mom.

To Katie and Oliver: The rest of us didn't have a choice, but you did! Thank you for being a part of the Brown family and its craziness.

To Kathy, Amy, Jen, Peggy, and Beth: Each one of you has upheld me. You have listened, shown up, given wise counsel, cried with me, and laughed with me. I consider you my sisters. I would not be who I am without you.

To Dr. Becky: Thank you for being adult supervision inside my head.

To my Friends University small group (salao chique): Thank you for your prayers and low-grade clowning. Your deep love for and commitment to Christ and others give me hope.

To my dear friends and cowriters, Carrie and Sara: I am privileged to be your friend and do this work with you. I love you both dearly.

From Carrie:

To my Savior: I wouldn't have chosen this path for my life, but I am grateful you did. I wouldn't be where I am today or know your love and care had you not intervened. You knew my independent heart and perfectly fashioned a life of dependence on you. Thank you.

To Bruce, my biggest cheerleader: When I wanted to sign up for that Mastermind, start a podcast, write a book, and fly to the ends of the earth, you didn't bat an eyelash. I'm grateful that you balance out my emotions and still carry Toby up six flights of stairs to zip-line. Our marriage is the 20 percent. Till death do us part.

To my children: I wouldn't trade homeschooling the last ten years for the world. I'm thrilled to see what God has planned for each of you. Conor, you're an amazing man, working hard and leading. Our relationship has turned from parent-child to friends. Garrett, you have a depth of care and empathy that I cherish. Your musical abilities amaze me. Toby, you've taught me more in your life than I've learned in mine. You bring joy to everyone you meet, and I'm grateful for your humor and love for others. Caris, you have the biggest heart and creative mind. One day you will be writing acknowledgments like this.

To my mom and dad: Thank you for bringing me up to walk in a true relationship with Jesus Christ, not based on rules or demands, for shaping my strong will so I could weather the storms of life, and for teaching me that God is faithful in all. I love you both.

To my sisters not only by birth but also by heart: You have loved, encouraged, and supported me, and you are steadfast examples of unconditional love. I love you and your families.

To my other parents, John and Lon Nell Holt: Thank you for being there in ways I can never repay. Thank you for treating me as a daughter. I'm grateful for "Do-we-spoil-'em-and-how" services.

To Erika, Jen P., and Sonya: Thank you for being the friends who "get" it. I don't have to explain; you just know. Your support, love, and advice have been a constant in my life.

To Mandy, Beth, Alisa, Jensine, Deb, and Alissa: You have given me the gifts of being honest and faithful; iron sharpens iron, my friends, and I'm grateful for all of you.

To Lifepoint Church, Dean and Angie, and so many others: Thank you for loving us, accepting us, and being the hands and feet of Jesus to our family. Marc Shields, I can't think about how you loved Toby before you barely knew him without tears. You are a light for Christ.

To Uncle Louis: Many years ago, you encouraged me to write a book. Thank you; here it is.

To the original Breath of Support Group: I couldn't have done those early years without you. You were an integral part of my connection and not walking this journey alone.

To Sara and Amy: It's hard to believe we haven't known each other our entire lives, because it sure feels like it. I'm grateful to do this sacred work with both of you. Love you both.

From Sara:

To Craig: You are my person. Thank you for your endless support. We met when we were just kids, and I am honored to have grown up with you. May we continue to grow old together. I'd do it all over again. Love infinity.

To Connor: Thank you for teaching me the joys of being a mom and humoring me through numerous mother-son dates. You are an amazing human. I'm honored to be your mom. I love you more than you could ever know.

To TJ: Your strength astounds me. There isn't a day that goes by that I don't thank God for your joy, your humor, and your grit. You are meant for great things. Three squeezes, for eternity.

To my mom, Terra: Thank you for introducing me to God. I am eternally grateful for your unconditional love, guidance, and encouragement. You have been and continue to be one of the strongest women I know.

To my sister, Emily: You'd be my best friend anyway. You are my *ride or die*, and I love you for exactly the person you are.

To Edie and Kyle, my girls, the daughters of my heart: You make me want to be better. Shine on!

To my other mom, Kay: Your support for our family and your excellent backup caregiving skills know no bounds. Thank you for being you. Love you always.

To Grandma Doris and Grandpa Terry: Grandma, thank you for being the first to instill the love of the written word into the fabric of my soul and for giving me permission to embrace my inner nerd. I miss you. Grandpa, thank you for my humor, entrepreneurial spirit, and strong work ethic. You held each of us to a higher standard and set the example of how to reach it. I love you.

To Liz and Greg: Hundreds of miles and time never seem to alter the strength of our bond. We love you both. Where's the next vacation?

To Robin K.: The hours of laughs, tears, and prayers have been a true gift. Thank you for always reflecting the love of Jesus.

To Nancy H.: Thank you for unraveling the knots and for protecting and nurturing the sacred spaces within. You are loved. You are family.

To Larry and Delores: You are a treasure, and God knew we needed you. You selflessly share your story to help mend others' hearts and point them to the love of Jesus. Thank you for your trusted counsel, always.

To our Capital City Christian Church family: Not only did you surround our family with endless love and support from day one but you also have helped create a safe space for other families like ours in our community. You are a city set on a hill that cannot be hidden.

To our City Champions: We are beyond honored to be doing life with each of you.

To my Central Christian College of the Bible master's program professors, leaders, and fellow students: Thank you for your prayers, the laughs, and for believing in me.

To my friends, cohosts, and cowriters, Amy and Carrie: Thank you both for sharing your lives, dreams, tears, and hope-filled words with me. I can't imagine doing life without you. I love you both.

Notes

Chapter 2 Grief to Hope

1. Cheri Fuller and Louise Tucker Jones, *Extraordinary Kids: Nurturing and Championing Your Child with Special Needs* (Colorado Springs: Focus on the Family, 1997), 33–34.

2. Cheri Fuller and Louise Tucker Jones, *Extraordinary Kids*, 33–34.

3. Adam Young, "Why Your Story Makes It Hard to Hope," episode 18, *The Place We Find Ourselves*, audio podcast, August 6, 2018, https://podcasts.apple.com/us/podcast/why-your-story-makes-it-hard-to-hope/id1373926216?i=1000417281411.

Chapter 3 Doubt to Faith

1. C. S. Lewis, *Letters of C. S. Lewis*, ed. W. H. Lewis (New York: HarperCollins, 1966, 1988), 610.

2. Jan Karon, *In This Mountain* (New York: Penguin Random House, 2003), 230.

3. Becky Davidson, "Carrie Holt: God Is in the Hard," episode 104, *Rising Above*, audio podcast, March 1, 2022, https://podcasts.apple.com/us/podcast/carrie-holt-god-is-in-the-hard/id1474115203?i=1000552542256.

4. David G. Benner, *The Gift of Being Yourself: The Sacred Call to Self-Discovery* (Downers Grove, IL: InterVarsity, 2015), 41.

Chapter 4 Comparison to Contentment

1. Ellie Sanazaro, "Interview with Ellie Sanazaro," episode 43, *Take Heart*, audio podcast, June 8, 2021, https://www.buzzsprout.com/1293716/8650035.

Chapter 5 Guilt to Acceptance

1. Brené Brown, "Brené Brown on the Difference between Guilt and Shame," Farnam Street, November 9, 2019, https://fs.blog/brene-brown -guilt-shame/.

2. Dictionary.com, s.v. "guilt," accessed May 3, 2022, https://www .dictionary.com/browse/guilt.

3. Brené Brown, *Daring Greatly: How the Courage to Be Vulnerable Transforms the Way We Live, Love, Parent, and Lead* (New York: Penguin Random House, 2012), 69.

4. Brown, *Daring Greatly*, 72.

Chapter 6 Anger to Comfort

1. Henri J. M. Nouwen, *Life of the Beloved: Spiritual Living in a Secular World* (Chestnut Ridge, PA: Crossroad Publishing Company, 1992), 78.

Chapter 7 Despair to Joy

1. *Anne of Green Gables*, directed by Kevin Sullivan (Toronto: Sullivan Entertainment Inc., 2006), DVD.

2. Dictionary.com, s.v. "despair," accessed March 20, 2022, https://www .dictionary.com/browse/despair.

3. Parker Palmer, *A Hidden Wholeness* (San Francisco: Jossey-Bass, 2004), 178.

4. S. D. Smith, *The Wreck and Rise of Whitson Mariner* (Beaver, WV: Story Warren Books, 2018), 54.

Chapter 8 Weariness to Rest

1. Ruth Haley Barton, *Invitation to Solitude and Silence: Experiencing God's Transforming Presence* (Downers Grove, IL: IVP Books, 2010), 58–59.

2. *Merriam-Webster*, s.v. "compassion fatigue," accessed April 30, 2022, https://www.merriam-webster.com/dictionary/compassion%20fatigue.

3. Barb Stanley, "Planting the Seeds For Kingdom Impact: An Interview with Barb Stanley," May 31, 2022, episode 88, *Take Heart*, audio podcast, 31:16, https://www.buzzsprout.com/1293716/10667760.

4. C. S. Lewis, *Letters of C. S. Lewis*, ed. W. H. Lewis (New York: HarperCollins, 1966, 1988), 499.

Chapter 9 Fear to Trust

1. Janet and Geoff Benge, *George Müller: The Guardian of Bristol's Orphans* (Seattle: YWAM, 1999), 168–69.

Chapter 11 Unexpected to Designed

1. Adrian Sandler, *Living With Spina Bifida* (Chapel Hill: University of North Carolina Press, 1997), 67–69.

Chapter 12 Disappointment to Gratitude

1. Kendra Adachi, *The Lazy Genius: Embrace What Matters, Ditch What Doesn't, and Get Stuff Done* (Colorado Springs: WaterBrook, 2020), 63.
2. Steve Saint, *End of the Spear* (Wheaton: Tyndale, 2005), 59–60.

Bonus Chapter: Navigating a Crisis

1. Dan Allender, "Vicarious Trauma and the Church," *Allender Center*, audio podcast, March 21, 2015, https://theallendercenter.org/2015/03/vicarious-trauma/.
2. Dictionary.com, s.v. "crisis," accessed April 27, 2022, https://www.dictionary.com/browse/crisis.

Amy J. Brown is a writer, mentor, and podcast host. She writes to encourage special needs moms. She shares honestly about adoption and parenting children with mental health issues and trauma. She believes that by sharing our stories we can learn from each other and be encouraged. But most importantly, we can feel less alone. She is the mother to six children. She lives with her husband in Michigan. You can find her online at www.amyjbrown.com.

Sara Clime is a writer, business owner, ministry leader, and podcast host. She writes and speaks with honesty, humor, and hope about the highs and lows of parenting a child with disabilities and complex medical needs. Sara's passion is to walk alongside other moms who may feel isolated, fearful, and defeated, eventually arriving at a place of community, feeling heard and seen, and ultimately authentic joy. Sara lives in Missouri with her husband and two children. You can find her online at www.saraclime.com.

Carrie M. Holt is a writer, speaker, and podcast host, encouraging special needs mothers to identify, accept, and thrive in the grieving cycle that is an ongoing part of this journey. She is also passionate about educating others regarding family-centered care and how to survive hospital stays. Carrie lives in Ohio with her husband and four children. You can find her online at www.carriemholt.com.